s'mores!

GOOEY, MELTY, CRUNCHY RIFFS ON THE CAMPFIRE CLASSIC

Dan Whalen

Workman Publishing • New York

Library of Congress Cataloging-in-Publication Data is available.

ISBN 978-1-5235-0433-6

Food stylist: Lori Powell
Prop stylist: Andrea Greco
Additional photos: Angela Cherry: cover (graham cracker); Food Collection RF/Getty: p. 46;
Shutterstock: pp. III, 17-19, 32-33, 93, 95, 107.

Workman books are available at special discounts when purchased in bulk for premiums
and sales promotions as well as for fund-raising or educational use. Special editions or
book excerpts can also be created to specification. For details, contact the Special Sales
Director at the address below, or send an email to specialmarkets@workman.com.

Workman Publishing Co., Inc.
225 Varick Street
New York, NY 10014-4381
workman.com

WORKMAN is a registered trademark of Workman Publishing Co., Inc.

Printed in China
First printing May 2019

10 9 8 7 6 5 4 3 2

The Rules of S'more

The culinary triad of graham cracker, marshmallow, and chocolate invites almost infinite adaptation. However, before we begin our journey through all of the possible variations of s'mores, it is important to set a few guidelines. Below are the general rules I followed when asking the ever-important question, "What is a s'more?" Like all rules, of course, I broke a few here and there, and I think you should, too.

❶ A s'more is **always a sandwich.** There are no s'mores-inspired desserts to be found here.

❷ Each s'more must have a **gooey, melty, and crunchy** element to it.

❸ If you start with graham cracker, marshmallow, and chocolate, **you can always add more to a s'more.**

❹ No matter how far away you get from the traditional s'more (and we get pretty far toward the end of the book), **your concoction must visually look like a s'more.** This usually means a couple of small square crackers or bread elements, with a white, round "thing" sandwiched in the middle.

❺ **Enjoy with friends!** Most of these recipes make twelve s'mores. That's for a reason.

the s'mores
FROM CLASSIC

S'MORE-O-METER

CLASSIC   CREATIVE   EDGY

...TO CRAZY

WILD   WHOA!   WHAT?

Introduction

Welcome to the crunchy, gooey, melty world of backyard bonfires and roasting sticks, of campfire songs and camaraderie. You will find nothing boring in this book of s'mores. It is simply a collection of riffs—from the expected to the outrageous—on one of the most beloved desserts of all time. Before you dive into the recipes, however, please pause to indulge me with a few pressing diversions . . .

What are s'mores?

S'mores have been, are, and always will be my favorite dessert. This traditional campfire treat is strikingly easy to put together—just graham crackers, chocolate, and marshmallow. That's it. And yet, these three simple ingredients have such staying power. I have countless memories of eating s'mores—the time, the place, and the friends I was with. Name any other dessert that's so simple and yet has such nostalgia attached to it!

Why is something so simple so amazing?

The flavors match perfectly. The flavors of the three simple ingredients just go so well together. The hint of salt in the graham cracker and the slight char on the marshmallow combine to make s'mores most people's first entry point into the world of salty desserts.

S'mores are texturally balanced. The best things come in threes, right? In this case, crunchy cracker, warm gooey marshmallow, and half-melted chocolate that coats your mouth.

S'mores are interactive. Instead of someone cooking behind closed doors and emerging with a finished cake, the creation of s'mores allows everyone to be involved in the fun! Each person thinks they make the perfect s'more, and everyone has their own method for toasting marshmallows. We will be introducing you to a handful of these toasting personalities throughout the book (pages 35, 52, 81, 107, 116, and 134).

S'mores are social. Bonfires and great conversations go hand in hand. And the competitive aspect of marshmallow toasting and s'more assembly can make things interesting.

You can eat them without shoes on. Anthony Bourdain (may he RIP) always said that food tastes better when your feet are in the sand. In this case, for "sand," just substitute grass or the ground near your fire pit. Eating outside surrounded by friends, nature, and a roaring fire creates a great atmosphere for enjoying food.

What are the s'mores in this book?

This book features fifty-one twists on the traditional s'mores package: a small sandwich with a crunchy exterior, creamy filling, and decadent sauce. The recipes start with classic and beloved dessert flavors. As you flip the pages, the ingredients move farther away from the norm, exchanging the usual trio for some wild s'mores ideas.

As the book progresses, the recipes gradually swap out the chocolate, graham cracker, and marshmallow, one by one, replacing each with similar textures and colors to see how far we can take the idea of s'mores without losing the recognizable components. When we start to vary flavors, we begin to rethink the true idea of what makes a s'more. By the end of the s'mores journey, the relationship to a traditional s'more is purely structural—it looks like a s'more, but doesn't taste like one! You can ride along on this quest—from classic to crazy—by starting at the beginning of the book and tasting the recipes in order, or hop around, looking for the flavor combinations that speak to you.

Because s'mores are so easy to make and so perfect as is, I made sure these recipes were mostly on the easy-to-make side. When they do get a little more challenging, they are very much worth the extra effort!

What you won't find in this book are s'mores flavors presented in a different format. For example, there are no s'mores cakes or s'mores cookies, just perfectly balanced stacks of ingredients.

Marshmallow Cooking

There are four main methods for cooking marshmallows to that perfect golden brown crust and gooey, melty middle. For purposes of this book, I wrote the recipes with the broiler method (following page) in mind, particularly for batches of twelve, but the best way will always be over an open fire. I encourage you to use the method that works best for you at the moment. Embrace the s'more year-round and try them all!

OVER THE FIRE
OVERALL WARMING: 1 foot above
PRECISION BROWNING ZONE: 2 to 4 inches away from an especially hot zone
EXTREME HEAT: in the actual flames

Whether it's flickering embers in a small pit or a huge blazing pyre, open flame is the classic s'mores heat source. Use a long-enough stick and find a spot near the fire that has a strong but medium temperature coming from multiple directions at the marshmallow. Keep a close eye on it to prevent burning on the outside (unless that's your thing) before the inside is warmed through. Experimentation is key.

GAS STOVETOP
OVERALL WARMING: 6 to 8 inches away
PRECISION BROWNING ZONE: 2 to 4 inches away

Using an uncovered gas burner on high heat is the way I initially toasted most of my marshmallows while creating these recipes. I like to hold the marshmallow high above the flame right in the center of the ring. If you hold it in the right spot, the heat becomes very concentrated. Keep spinning the marshmallow to avoid flare-ups and to get a nice even color and temperature.

COOKING TORCH

PRECISION BROWNING ZONE: 2 to 4 inches away

A cooking torch can be a nice way to get precise browning, but it is harder to achieve an overall cooked-through, gooey-in-the-middle marshmallow. So you don't burn the counter or a plate, put the marshmallow on a baking sheet oiled with cooking spray, and hold the torch far away to start so you can control the browning and internal temperature.

BROILER

PRECISION BROWNING ZONE: a rack in the upper third of the oven

The broiler method is used in the recipes in this book. Every broiler is different, so here are my general tips.

First, and this is true with broiling anything, you need to watch the marshmallows as they broil. Marshmallows can easily turn into tiny flaming pillows and, if you walk away for even a single minute, you might end up with an oven fire. The number one way to NOT have fun making s'mores is to set something ablaze that is not meant to be.

Second, test your broiler. A good way to do this is to fill a pan with marshmallows and place it under the broiler. Keep a close eye on it. After a few minutes you will clearly see the hot spots and cold spots based on the browning patterns on the marshmallows. You should keep those hot spots in mind when preparing your s'mores in the oven.

Third, place the rack as close to the broiler as it can go. This advice is the same whether you have a gas, electric, or drawer-style broiler.

Fourth, preheat the broiler. You may not think you need to preheat it, but just a few minutes of preheating with gas, and closer to ten minutes with electric, will help you get much better and more even results.

Fifth, again, depending on your oven, you might need to keep the oven door ajar. Some broilers shut off if the heat gets too intense in the oven; leaving the door cracked open will avoid this issue.

A Note on Chocolate

A typical chocolate bar is made up of 12 pips—the small rectangles that make it easy to break the bar into bite-sized shareable pieces. The standard for s'mores is Hershey's chocolate bars, so that is what I used in these recipes. I went a little lighter on the chocolate than what I have seen elsewhere because I think the ratio is better. Chocolate can easily overpower the other ingredients. It's really based on personal preference, though, so don't feel like you need to follow my lead. At any time, feel free to use any brand of milk chocolate or a darker variety that you like. Just don't use white chocolate, please.

Homemade Marshmallows

Homemade marshmallows are a different beast than their store-bought counterparts. If you have never made them, put this recipe on the top of your list. I am not saying you need to make them for every s'more—I absolutely don't—but when you do use them, it makes everything that much more special. The best time to make them is near the holidays, since they keep well and are great to have on hand for hot chocolate. And if you are going through the effort of making them, why not add in flavors? I have given a few suggestions after this recipe, but the possibilities are endless.

Makes 36 🔥 Takes 30 minutes active time, 6 hours total

¾ cup water

3 tablespoons gelatin (usually three 7-gram packages)

2 cups granulated sugar

½ cup corn syrup or agave nectar

Pinch of kosher salt

1 tablespoon pure vanilla extract

½ cup cornstarch

1½ cups confectioners' sugar

About 2 tablespoons butter, or another solid fat, such as shortening or coconut oil, plus more for the knife

- -

1   Place ½ cup of the water in the bowl of a stand mixer fitted with the whisk attachment, or in a large bowl. Add the gelatin and stir. Let the mixture sit so the gelatin can bloom, about 5 minutes. You'll know it's blooming when the water reaches a gel-like consistency.

2   Meanwhile, combine the granulated sugar, corn syrup, salt, and remaining ¼

cup of water in a small saucepan. Stir well to mix. Place the pan over medium heat and cook, stirring, until the sugar dissolves.

3   Attach a candy thermometer to the saucepan (do not let it touch the bottom) and turn the heat to high. Cook, undisturbed, until the temperature reaches 245°F, or the soft-ball stage (meaning if you were to squeeze the syrup mixture when cool, it would be only slightly pliable). Remove from the heat.

4   Using the stand mixer or a handheld electric mixer, whisk the gelatin mixture on medium speed. Slowly pour the hot sugar mixture down the side of the bowl into the gelatin mixture. Once added, turn the speed to high and whisk until the mixture is light and fluffy, 5 to 7 minutes. In the last minute of mixing, add the salt and vanilla.

5   Mix the cornstarch and confectioners' sugar in a medium bowl.

6   Grease a deep 8-by-8-inch baking pan with a thin layer of butter. Coat it with ½ cup of the cornstarch mixture, knocking out any excess.

7   Pour the marshmallow mixture into the prepared pan. Top the marshmallows with another ½ cup of the cornstarch mixture. Let the marshmallows sit, uncovered, on the counter to set, at least 6 hours.

8   Lightly dust your work surface with some of the cornstarch mixture. Turn the marshmallows out onto the dusted surface.

9   Grease a knife with butter. Cut the marshmallows to make 6 rows of 6 marshmallows, a total of 36.

10   Coat each marshmallow one more time in the cornstarch mixture. Place the marshmallows in an airtight container until ready to use. They will keep at room temperature for at least a month.

Mallow Mash-Ups

Replace the vanilla extract with 1 scraped vanilla bean pod.

Replace the vanilla extract with a few drops of peppermint extract.

Add 2 teaspoons ground cinnamon with the salt and vanilla in Step 4.

Add ¼ cup cocoa powder with the salt and vanilla in Step 4.

Stir in ½ cup toasted coconut flakes with the salt and vanilla in Step 4.

THE HISTORY OF THE MOST BELOVED CAMPFIRE TREAT

2000 BC

EGYPT
Mother of Marshmallows!

Ancient Egyptians extracted mallow sap from the root of the marshmallow plant (*Althaea officinalis*), and mixed it with nuts and honey. The result was a treat so delightful it was reserved as a delicacy for the pharaohs and the gods.

1900 BC

SOUTH AND CENTRAL AMERICAS
Drink of the Gods

The indigenous peoples of South and Central America are believed to be the first to discover that the beans of the cacao (or cocoa) plant could be harvested and made into liquid gold—chocolate. The various drinks made from the cacao bean were used in ritual celebrations and as currency.

4TH CENTURY

GREECE
Mallow as Herbal Remedy

Mallow sap is found in the fourth-century medicinal recipes of Hippocrates for relief of swelling and inflammation.

19TH CENTURY

FRANCE
The French Find a Way

Marshmallow as candy resurfaced in nineteenth-century France, when confectioners took a mixture of the sap, syrup, whipped egg whites, and orange flower water, and turned it into a treat closely resembling the distinct cube-like shape of today's marshmallow. Surprisingly, the modern, store-bought marshmallow contains no mallow sap. Extraction proved to be too expensive and laborious, so gelatin became a worthy substitute.

1837
CONNECTICUT
Graham's Moral Cracker
A radical New England reverend, Sylvester Graham, blamed the carnal appetites of Americans on white flour. He encouraged his followers to grow their own wheat and developed a process for making his own flour. That flour was used to make Graham bread and the more well-known Graham cracker.

1847
BRISTOL, ENGLAND
The Molten Liquid Cools
The Fry brothers of J. S. Fry & Sons—a family owned chocolate producer in England—are believed to have invented the first mass-produced chocolate bar. They created a paste of cocoa powder, sugar, and cocoa fat that could be formed into a bar. Prior to their invention, chocolate was only consumed as a drink.

1893
HERSHEY, PENNSYLVANIA
Chocolate Made Accessible
We can thank the 1893 Columbian Exposition in Chicago for Hershey's chocolate. Formerly a producer of caramels, Milton Hershey was awestruck by a demonstration of German chocolate manufacturing machinery, declaring "caramels are a fad but chocolate is permanent." Hershey's was the first to mass-produce chocolate bars in the United States, adding milk from local dairy farms to give it a smooth, creamy taste.

1925
USA
May I Have Some More?
The earliest known version of the s'mores recipe was printed in a 1925 issue of *Girl Scout Leader* magazine and then again as "Somemores" in a 1927 Girl Scout publication called *Tramping and Trailing with the Girl Scouts*.

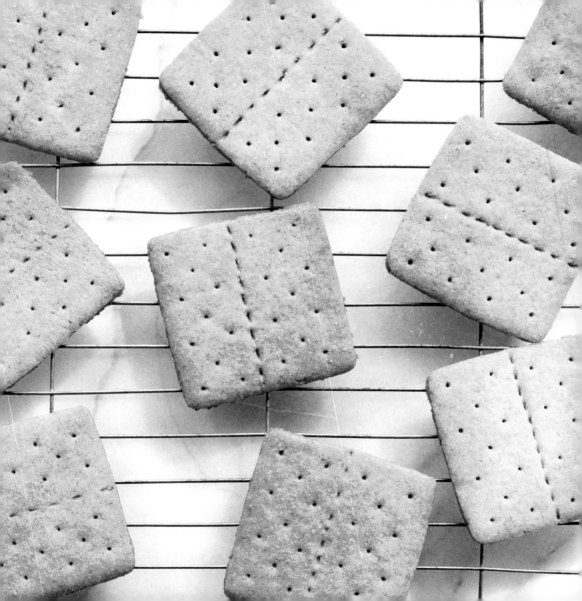

Homemade Honey Graham Crackers

J ust like homemade marshmallows, from-scratch graham crackers are a great way to make your s'mores special. These taste so good that it's hard not to eat half of them straight out of the oven! I cut these a little smaller than store-bought grahams because they end up a little thicker, and I think it helps the s'mores ratio. If you are making them for the Huge S'mores on page 84, the thickness will help the two huge crackers remain sturdy.

Makes 32 crackers (2 inches square) 🔥 **Takes 30 minutes active time, 2 hours total**

1½ cups all-purpose flour, plus
   more for the work surface
1¼ cups graham flour or whole-wheat
   flour
1 teaspoon baking soda

1 teaspoon kosher salt
1 cup (2 sticks) unsalted butter,
   at room temperature
½ cup packed dark brown sugar
¼ cup honey

. . . .

1 Mix the flours, baking soda, and salt together in a large bowl.

2 Combine the butter, brown sugar, and honey in another large bowl. Using a handheld electric mixer, beat until light and fluffy, about 3 minutes.

3 Add the flour mixture to the butter mixture. Beat until combined, about 1 minute. Form the dough into a 1-inch-thick disk and wrap it in plastic wrap. Refrigerate for at least 1 hour.

4 Place a rack in the upper third of the oven and another in the lower third and preheat the oven to 350°F. Line two baking sheets with parchment paper or silicone baking mats and set aside.

5 Lightly flour a work surface. Unwrap the dough, place it on the floured surface, and roll it out to about ⅛-inch thickness. Cut the dough into about 32 two-inch squares. Using a toothpick, score a line down the middle of each square and make 11 holes on each side in the traditional graham pattern.

6 Place the squares on the prepared baking sheets. Bake, rotating the sheets front to back and top rack to bottom rack about halfway through the cooking time, until golden brown and slightly firm to the touch, about 15 minutes. Remove from the oven and let cool for at least 15 minutes before using. The graham crackers will keep in an airtight container at room temperature for up to a week.

Do It for the Graham

Add ½ teaspoon ground cinnamon to the dry ingredients in Step 1.

Add ¼ teaspoon ground cinnamon and ¼ teaspoon ground cloves to the dry ingredients in Step 1, and use molasses instead of honey.

Add ½ teaspoon chai spice to the dry ingredients in Step 1.

Replace ½ cup all-purpose flour with ½ cup cocoa powder.

Omit 4 tablespoons (½ stick) unsalted butter and add ½ cup peanut butter instead.

Classic S'mores

How could we start a book on s'mores without a visit to the hallowed ground of the basic trio? Here, I'm using homemade marshmallows and graham crackers to get that extra handmade, cozy feeling. But if you don't have time to invest in preparing those ingredients, just go with store-bought. No judgment.

Makes 12 🔥 Takes 10 minutes

Nonstick cooking spray
24 squares of Homemade Honey Graham
  Crackers (page 15)

2 bars (1.55 ounces each) milk chocolate,
  broken into individual pips
12 Homemade Marshmallows (page 9)

1   Place a rack in the upper third of the oven and turn the broiler to its highest setting. Preheat for 5 to 10 minutes. Spray a baking sheet with cooking spray.

2   Place 12 graham cracker squares on a serving platter. Top each square with 2 chocolate pips and set aside.

3   Place the marshmallows on the prepared baking sheet. Broil them until they're golden brown on top, about 3 minutes. Keep a close eye on them.

4   Place 1 toasted marshmallow on each s'more. Top the s'mores with the remaining graham cracker squares and serve immediately.

MAKE YOUR OWN S'MORES PARTY!

Even though all you need to make s'mores indoors is an oven (and occasionally a stovetop), the recipes in this book can be toted outside very easily. Many of them require little to no prep. Start with the basics and build your s'mores kit with as many of these portable wildcards as you want:

① FIRE

② STICKS

③ FIRE EXTINGUISHER

④ FRIENDS

⑤ THE BIG THREE
chocolate
graham crackers
marshmallows

⑥ WILDCARDS

- Almonds
- Avocado
- Banana
- Blue cheese
- Brie
- Cheesecake
- Chocolate chip cookies
- Cookie dough
- Fig jam
- Fresh herbs, such as basil or mint
- Nutella
- Oreo cookies
- Peaches
- Peanut butter
- Peanut butter cups or other flat candy
- Pizzelles
- Potato chips
- Pretzels
- Salted caramel
- Shortbread cookies
- Sprinkles
- Sriracha
- Toasted coconut

the recipes

FROM CLASSIC TO CRAZY

Peanut Butter Cup S'mores

A piece of semi-melted chocolate is usually the glue in the middle of the traditional gooey and crunchy s'mores components. But . . . why not swap in another type of chocolate (candy!) between that graham cracker and marshmallow? Here, I went for the classic peanut-butter-and-chocolate combo, but why stop there? Take a look at the box for ideas on other kinds of candy that would make a great twist on a s'more.

Makes 12 🔥 Takes 10 minutes

Nonstick cooking spray
12 whole graham crackers, broken in half to form 24 squares

12 peanut butter cups
12 regular marshmallows

- -

1   Place a rack in the upper third of the oven and turn the broiler to its highest setting. Preheat for 5 to 10 minutes. Spray a baking sheet with cooking spray.

2   Place 12 graham cracker squares on the prepared baking sheet. Top each square with 1 peanut butter cup. Squish each marshmallow a bit with your hands and place 1 marshmallow on each peanut

butter cup. Broil the s'mores until the marshmallows are golden brown on top, about 3 minutes. Keep a close eye on them.

3   Transfer the s'mores to a serving dish and top with the remaining graham cracker squares. Serve immediately.

CANDY BAR S'MORES!

The candy bar options for s'mores go way beyond chocolate bars and peanut butter cups. Here are some other options that work great—but let your imagination run wild! Depending on what you use, just cut it to fit the s'more. I like to let the thicker candy bars melt for a minute in a warm oven right on the graham cracker and smoosh them down a bit before adding the marshmallow.

BUTTERFINGER

CHOCOLATE BARK

CRUNCH

KIT KAT

MILKY WAY

MOUNDS

PEPPERMINT PATTIES

SNICKERS

TAKE5

TWIX

WHATCHAMACALLIT

PB&J S'mores

S'mores aren't the only childhood favorites that come in the form of a conveniently packaged sandwich. Being from New England, I put Fluff in my PB&J, so it was practically a s'more already. (Fun fact: Fluff was invented in Somerville, MA, and the Fluffernutter has been proposed as the official state sandwich of Massachusetts.) These PB&J s'mores taste like memories. The melty peanut butter and jelly make this one of the stickiest s'mores of the bunch, but you will be licking the happy mess off your hands with a smile. **Makes 12** 🔥 **Takes 10 minutes**

Nonstick cooking spray

12 whole graham crackers, broken in half
   to form 24 squares

¾ cup creamy peanut butter

2 bars (1.55 ounces each) milk chocolate,
   broken into individual pips

12 regular marshmallows

½ cup of your favorite jelly
   (I like strawberry.)

1   Place a rack in the upper third of the oven and turn the broiler to its highest setting. Preheat for 5 to 10 minutes. Spray a baking sheet with cooking spray.

2   Place 12 graham cracker squares on the prepared baking sheet. Spread about 1 tablespoon of peanut butter on each cracker.

3   Top each square with 2 chocolate pips. Squish each marshmallow a bit with your hands and place 1 marshmallow on each s'more. Broil the s'mores until the marshmallows are golden brown on top, about 3 minutes. Keep a close eye on them.

4   Transfer the s'mores to a serving dish. Top each marshmallow with about 2 teaspoons of jelly and another graham cracker square. Serve immediately.

Nutella S'mores

I love the complex s'mores in this book so much, but it's really hard to beat anything with Nutella in it. This s'more is simpler than many of the other recipes, but something about that creamy Italian chocolate–hazelnut spread is magic. You don't want to add too much more to it. **Makes 12** 🔥 **Takes 10 minutes**

Nonstick cooking spray
12 whole graham crackers, broken in half
    to form 24 squares

¾ cup chocolate-hazelnut spread, such
    as Nutella
12 regular marshmallows

1 Place a rack in the upper third of the oven and turn the broiler to its highest setting. Preheat for 5 to 10 minutes. Spray a baking sheet with cooking spray.

2 Place 12 graham cracker squares on the prepared baking sheet. Top each square with 1 tablespoon of chocolate-hazelnut spread. Squish each marshmallow a bit with your hands and place 1 marshmallow on each s'more. Broil the s'mores until the marshmallows are golden brown on top, about 3 minutes. Keep a close eye on them.

3 Transfer the s'mores to a serving dish and top with the remaining graham cracker squares. Serve immediately.

Ice Cream
S'morewiches

Ice cream is one of the most universally beloved summer treats. Turns out, this perfect little ice cream s'morewich works well with lots of different flavors in addition to vanilla. My favorite is mint cookies and cream, but coffee, strawberry, butter pecan, and peanut butter ripple all taste awesome. It's fine to wait a few minutes after getting the ice cream out of the freezer so that it's more scoopable, as long as you will eat the s'morewich right away. **Makes 12** ⚜ **Takes 10 minutes**

Nonstick cooking spray

12 whole graham crackers, broken in half to form 24 squares

2 bars (1.55 ounces each) milk chocolate, broken into individual pips

12 regular marshmallows

¾ cup vanilla ice cream

¼ cup rainbow sprinkles

12 maraschino cherries (optional)

1 Place a rack in the upper third of the oven and turn the broiler to its highest setting. Preheat for 5 to 10 minutes. Spray a baking sheet with cooking spray.

2 Place 12 graham cracker squares on a serving platter. Top each square with 2 chocolate pips and set aside.

3 Place the marshmallows on the prepared baking sheet. Broil them until they're golden brown on top, about 3 minutes. Keep a close eye on them.

4 When the marshmallows are done, top the chocolate with 1 heaping tablespoon of ice cream and 1 teaspoon of sprinkles.

5 Place 1 toasted marshmallow on each s'more. Top the s'mores with the remaining graham cracker squares and the maraschino cherries, if desired. Serve immediately.

Salted Caramel
S'mores

The first time I tasted salted caramel, it was a game changer for me. I consider it to be a real entry point for people when it comes to combining salty and sweet foods and getting more adventurous with desserts. I'm excited to introduce you to this foolproof recipe for salted caramel—it's really tasty, and it's perfect for drizzling on a classic s'more. **Makes 12 🔥 Takes 25 minutes, plus 1 hour to rest**

For the salted caramel sauce
1 cup sugar

4 tablespoons (½ stick) unsalted butter, at room temperature, cut into 4 pieces

½ cup heavy (whipping) cream

1 teaspoon kosher salt

For the s'mores
Nonstick cooking spray

12 whole graham crackers, broken in half to form 24 squares

2 bars (1.55 ounces each) milk chocolate, broken into individual pips

12 regular marshmallows

1   Place the sugar in a medium saucepan over high heat and whisk as it begins to melt. It will form clumps first, but eventually will become liquid, about 5 minutes.

2   Stop whisking and continue to cook the sugar, gently swirling the pan occasionally, until it turns a deep amber color, about 3 minutes more.

3   Add the butter. Whisk until it's melted, about 1 minute—the caramel will bubble up rapidly during this step. Remove the mixture from the heat and whisk in the cream. The sauce will be opaque, thick, and slightly lightened in color from the butter and cream. Add the salt and whisk to combine. Pour the caramel sauce into a jar and let it cool in the refrigerator for

an hour before you prepare the remaining ingredients. As it cools it will thicken more, but will stay pourable.

4 Place a rack in the upper third of the oven and turn the broiler to its highest setting. Preheat for 5 to 10 minutes. Spray a baking sheet with cooking spray.

5 Place 12 graham cracker squares on the prepared baking sheet. Top each square with 2 chocolate pips. Squish each marshmallow a bit with your hands and place 1 marshmallow on each s'more. Broil the s'mores until the marshmallows are golden brown on top, about 3 minutes. Keep a close eye on them.

6 Transfer the s'mores to a serving dish. Drizzle the salted caramel sauce on the toasted marshmallows and top with the remaining graham cracker squares. Serve immediately.

GOOEY, MELTY, CRUNCHY HOLIDAYS

Although every day is a day for s'mores (especially now that we know how easy it is to make them indoors), here are a few key dates for those wishing for a bit more s'mores fanfare. Mark your calendar for these important holidays:

July 5	National Graham Cracker Day
July 7	World Chocolate Day
August 10	National S'mores Day
August 30	National Toasted Marshmallow Day
October 28	National Chocolate Day

Berry Banana
S'mores

Most of my favorite breakfasts include bananas and strawberries. The combination of sweet and tart—plus the feeling that I'm eating healthy—is always a winner for me. That's why when I eat bananas for dessert I need to brown them first to bring out that sugary caramelization. The fire adds a nice charred flavor and slightly crunchy crust to complement burned marshmallows in a s'more. **Makes 12 🔥 Takes 15 minutes**

Nonstick cooking spray

12 whole graham crackers, broken in half to form 24 squares

3 large strawberries, hulled, each sliced into 8 thin rounds

2 bars (1.55 ounces each) milk chocolate, broken into individual pips

2 very ripe (almost 50 percent blackened) bananas, each cut into 6 pieces

Pinch of kosher salt

Pinch of sugar

12 regular marshmallows

. . . .

1 Place a rack in the upper third of the oven and turn the broiler to its highest setting. Preheat for 5 to 10 minutes. Spray a baking sheet with cooking spray.

2 Place 12 graham cracker squares on a large plate. Top each square with 2 strawberry slices, followed by 2 chocolate pips.

3 Place the bananas on the prepared baking sheet. Sprinkle with the salt and sugar. Broil the bananas until they start to brown, about 5 minutes.

4 Squish each marshmallow a bit with your hands, place on top of the bananas, and return the baking sheet to the broiler until the marshmallows are golden brown, about 3 minutes more. Keep a close eye on them.

5 Place 1 toasted marshmallow and 1 charred banana piece on each s'more. Top the s'mores with the remaining graham cracker squares. Serve immediately.

A Graham of Chance

If you've set up a s'mores bar with lots of different add-ins and ingredients, why not add a fun game to the festivities? Assign each ingredient a card number. Each person chooses his or her two stable ingredients (e.g., marshmallow, chocolate, or graham cracker) and for the third, draws from the deck!

Cookie Dough
S'mores

I used to work in a gelato shop where the owner was always hesitant to put American flavors, like cookie dough, on the menu. He wanted to stay authentic to traditional Italian gelato, while I generally swayed more toward, "Why not give the people what they want?" When I made this cookie dough mixture as a test run, though, there was no more debate. We both loved it and put it on the menu the next day!

You should have exactly the right amount of cookie dough to be able to snack on some as you add heaping tablespoons to the s'mores. If you somehow do end up with extra dough, it will keep in the refrigerator, wrapped tightly in plastic wrap, for up to two weeks. **Makes 12 🔥 Takes 25 minutes**

¾ cup all-purpose flour

5 tablespoons unsalted butter, at room
    temperature

¼ cup packed dark brown sugar

⅓ cup granulated sugar

2 tablespoons whole milk

½ teaspoon pure vanilla extract

¼ cup mini chocolate chips

Nonstick cooking spray

12 whole graham crackers, broken in half
    to form 24 squares

12 regular marshmallows

1 Toast the flour in a dry frying pan over medium high heat to darken it slightly in color, about 5 minutes. Stir occasionally.

2 Place the butter and sugars in a large bowl and beat to combine using a handheld electric mixer, about 2 minutes.

Stir in the toasted flour, milk, vanilla, and chocolate chips. Set the dough aside at room temperature.

3   Place a rack in the upper third of the oven and turn the broiler to its highest setting. Preheat for 5 to 10 minutes. Spray a baking sheet with cooking spray.

4   Place 12 graham cracker squares on the prepared baking sheet. Top each square with 1 heaping tablespoon of cookie dough. Squish each marshmallow a bit with your hands and place 1 marshmallow on each spoonful of cookie dough. Broil the s'mores until the marshmallows are golden brown on top, about 3 minutes. Keep a close eye on them.

5   Transfer the s'mores to a serving dish and top with the remaining graham cracker squares. Serve immediately.

The Various Personalities of

MARSHMALLOW ROASTERS

1

THE COUCH-MALLOW

is relaxing and doesn't need to be bothered with cooking a marshmallow properly. This person will try to find a hole in the rocks or a place in the dirt to stick the other end of the stick and allow the marshmallow to warm slowly, safely away from the real heat of the fire. When either they finally remember the marshmallow, or it appears to be falling off the stick, they will collect it and make their s'more. (Or, they'll find the marshmallow on the ground and have to restart.)

Peppermint S'mores

Because candy canes are such a Christmasy thing, these peppermint s'mores definitely have a holiday vibe going on. But just as we should embrace the year-round s'more, I see no reason why the combo of peppermint and chocolate should remain seasonal. Go ahead—make these at any time of year! Try chocolate mint cookies instead of graham crackers if you want to go the extra minty mile. **Makes 12 ⚶ Takes 10 minutes**

Nonstick cooking spray

6 individually wrapped peppermint candies

12 whole graham crackers, broken in half to form 24 squares

12 regular marshmallows

2 bars (1.55 ounces each) milk chocolate, broken into individual pips

1 Place a rack in the upper third of the oven and turn the broiler to its highest setting. Preheat for 5 to 10 minutes. Spray a baking sheet with cooking spray.

2 On a cutting board, using the side of a knife or a cooking mallet, smash the still-wrapped peppermint candies to shatter them. Remove them from the plastic wrappers and place the peppermint shards in a small bowl.

3 Place 12 graham cracker squares on the prepared baking sheet. Top each square with 2 chocolate pips and 1 teaspoon of peppermint shards. Squish each marshmallow a bit with your hands and place 1 marshmallow on each s'more. Broil until the marshmallows are golden brown on top, about 3 minutes. Keep a close eye on them.

4 Transfer the s'mores to a serving dish and top with the remaining graham cracker squares. Serve immediately.

Cake Batter S'mores

For this recipe, I figured out the absolute simplest way to approximate cake batter with no raw eggs and just 3 ingredients! If the batter feels too soft in Step 2, add more wafers to the food processor. Any leftover batter will keep in an airtight container in the refrigerator for 2 days. **Makes 12** 🔥 **Takes 20 minutes**

Nonstick cooking spray

1½ cups vanilla wafer cookies

6 ounces (¾ cup) cream cheese
    (from a tub, not a brick)

¼ cup rainbow sprinkles

12 whole graham crackers, broken in half
    to form 24 squares

2 bars (1.55 ounces each) milk chocolate,
    broken into individual pips

12 regular marshmallows

. . . .

1   Place a rack in the upper third of the oven and turn the broiler to its highest setting. Preheat for 5 to 10 minutes. Spray a baking sheet with cooking spray.

2   In a food processor, grind the cookies into a powder. Add the cream cheese and process until smooth. Transfer the cake batter to a medium bowl. Stir in 2 tablespoons of sprinkles.

3   Place 12 graham cracker squares on a serving dish. Top each square with 2 chocolate pips, 1 heaping

tablespoon of cake batter, and some of the rainbow sprinkles from the remaining 2 tablespoons.

4   Place the marshmallows on the prepared baking sheet. Broil them until they're golden brown on top, about 3 minutes. Keep a close eye on them.

5   Place 1 toasted marshmallow on each s'more. Top the s'mores with the remaining graham cracker squares. Serve immediately.

Banoffee S'mores

Banoffee pie is a British dessert of banana and toffee that has been taking the internet—and the world—by storm. The pie crust is made of crushed digestive cookies, which, when whole, just happen to be the perfect size to replace the graham cracker in a s'more. **Makes 12 🔥 Takes 15 minutes**

Nonstick cooking spray

24 digestive cookies, such as McVitie's

4 bars (1.55 ounces each) milk chocolate, broken into individual pips

2 very ripe bananas, each cut into 12 slices

½ cup toffee bits

12 regular marshmallows

- -

1 Place a rack in the upper third of the oven and turn the broiler to its highest setting. Preheat for 5 to 10 minutes. Spray a baking sheet with cooking spray.

2 Place 12 digestive cookies on a large serving dish. Top each cookie with 4 chocolate pips, 2 banana slices, and about 2 teaspoons of toffee pieces.

3 Place the marshmallows on the prepared baking sheet. Broil them until they're golden brown on top, about 3 minutes. Keep a close eye on them.

4 Place 1 toasted marshmallow on each s'more. Top the s'mores with the remaining digestive cookies. Serve immediately.

Caramel Apple S'mores

Caramel apples are my least favorite dessert. They are so messy and the ratios are all wrong—so much stickiness from the caramel melting off and a massive amount of apple to get through at the end. Translate those flavors into a s'more, though, and the ratio is perfect—I am all in! **Makes 12 🔥 Takes 15 minutes**

Nonstick cooking spray

12 whole graham crackers, broken in half to form 24 squares

2 medium apples, each cut into about 18 very thin wedges (use your favorite— I like Honeycrisp.)

¾ cup Salted Caramel Sauce (page 29)

12 regular marshmallows

. . . .

1 Place a rack in the upper third of the oven and turn the broiler to its highest setting. Preheat for 5 to 10 minutes. Spray a baking sheet with cooking spray.

2 Place 12 graham cracker squares on the prepared baking sheet. Top each square with 2 or 3 apple wedges and drizzle 1 tablespoon of caramel sauce over each s'more.

3 Squish each marshmallow a bit with your hands and place 1 marshmallow on each s'more. Broil the s'mores until the marshmallows are golden brown on top, about 3 minutes. Keep a close eye on them.

4 Transfer the s'mores to a serving dish and top with the remaining graham cracker squares. Serve immediately.

Toasted Coconut S'mores

Toasted coconut is one of my favorite dessert flavors, but it can be finicky to make. It can go from perfectly toasted to burned in seconds! That shouldn't stop you from making these, though, because I'm providing a pan-toasting method, and the flavor of the browned coconut goes so well with the marshmallow and chocolate. If you want to take it a step further, add Salted Caramel Sauce (page 29) and these will taste like the caramel-coconut Girl Scout cookies everyone loves. Just make sure to keep a close eye on the toasting coconut so you don't end up with burned bits.

Makes 12 🔥 Takes 20 minutes

Nonstick cooking spray

2 cups sweetened shredded coconut

1 tablespoon coconut oil, at room
  temperature

12 whole graham crackers, broken
  in half to form 24 squares

2 bars (1.55 ounces each) milk chocolate,
  broken into individual pips

12 regular marshmallows

. . . .

1   Preheat the oven to 350°F, with a rack in the top position. Line one baking sheet with parchment paper or a silicone baking mat and spray the other with cooking spray. Set the sprayed baking sheet aside.

2   Place the coconut on the prepared baking sheet lined with parchment paper and add the coconut oil. Mix together so the oil is evenly incorporated. Bake until the coconut is perfectly golden, about 12 minutes, stirring every 2 minutes for even toasting. Check for over-browning as you stir and take the pan out of the oven if the coconut becomes too brown throughout. Transfer the baking sheet to a wire rack to let it cool.

3 Using oven mitts, place a rack in the upper third of the oven and turn the broiler to its highest setting. Preheat for 5 to 10 minutes.

4 Place 12 graham cracker squares on the sprayed baking sheet. Top each square with 2 chocolate pips, followed by 1 heaping tablespoon of toasted coconut. Squish each marshmallow a bit with

your hands and place 1 marshmallow on each s'more. Broil the s'mores until the marshmallows are golden brown on top, about 3 minutes. Keep a close eye on them.

5 Transfer the s'mores to a serving dish and top with the remaining graham cracker squares and more toasted coconut, as desired. Serve immediately.

THE GRAHAM DIET PLAN

Reverend Sylvester Graham, a nineteenth-century New England Presbyterian minister who was obsessed with self-improvement in the most Puritanical of ways, is credited with the invention of the graham cracker. In 1837, Graham published *A Treatise on Bread and Bread-Making,* a book that was said to have a wide-reaching and influential impact on modern America's dietary and hygienic habits. It pushed a plant-based diet and regular exercise, and blamed carnal appetites (which Graham claimed led to disease) on meat and alcohol consumption. He labeled bread as particularly "vile" due to the use of white flour, which is devoid of all of wheat's nutrients, and urged his followers to grow their own wheat and mill their own flour. Much like the whole-grain variety, Graham's recipe for flour retained the bran and germ, and was unsifted, leading to a much coarser texture. The flour came to be known as Graham flour—it was used to make Graham bread and eventually the Graham cracker.

Crispy Treat S'mores

Because crispy rice treats are pretty much 50 percent marshmallow, this is literally serving marshmallow on top of marshmallow. How could you go wrong? **Makes 12 ⚲ Takes 30 minutes**

6 cups crispy rice cereal

4 tablespoons (½ stick) unsalted butter

52 regular marshmallows

2 bars (1.55 ounces each) milk chocolate, broken into individual pips

Nonstick cooking spray

1 Place a large rectangle of parchment paper on the work surface. Pour the cereal into a large mixing bowl.

2 Melt the butter in a large saucepan over medium heat. Add 40 of the marshmallows and stir constantly until they melt, 3 to 5 minutes.

3 Pour the melted marshmallows into the bowl with the cereal and mix well. Spoon the cereal mixture onto the parchment and flatten it with a spatula. Top with another piece of parchment. Using a rolling pin, roll out the treats to ¾-inch thickness. Remove the top piece of parchment and slice the treats into 24 two-inch squares.

4 Transfer 12 squares to a serving dish. Top each square with 2 chocolate pips.

5 Place a rack in the upper third of the oven and turn the broiler to its highest setting. Preheat for 5 to 10 minutes. Spray a baking sheet with cooking spray.

6 Place the remaining 12 marshmallows on the prepared baking sheet. Broil them until they're golden brown on top, about 3 minutes. Keep a close eye on them.

7 Place 1 toasted marshmallow on each s'more. Top the s'mores with the remaining cereal squares. Serve immediately.

Baklava S'mores

Crispy phyllo dough makes a light and balanced replacement for the graham crackers in this s'more. Honey, pistachio butter, and mini chocolate chips really make it taste like baklava!

Makes 12 🔥 Takes 30 minutes

1 cup (2 sticks) unsalted
    butter, melted
12 whole sheets phyllo dough
2 cups shelled, roasted, and
    salted pistachios
½ cup honey

Kosher salt
1 teaspoon peanut oil
Nonstick cooking spray
¾ cup mini chocolate chips
12 regular marshmallows

1 Preheat the oven to 450°F, with a rack in the middle position.

2 Brush a baking sheet with a little bit of the melted butter and place a single sheet of phyllo dough on it. Brush the dough evenly with a little more butter. Repeat until all 12 sheets are stacked and brushed with butter. Using a pizza cutter, gently cut the phyllo stack into 24 two-and-a-half-inch squares—roughly the size of graham cracker squares. Bake the phyllo until crispy, about 12 minutes. Separate the phyllo squares so they aren't touching each other and transfer them to a wire rack to cool.

3 Place the pistachios into a food processor and pulse for 30 seconds to break them up a bit. Add the honey, a pinch of salt, and the peanut oil. Process until the mixture forms a paste, about 1 minute, pausing to scrape down the sides, if needed.

4 Using oven mitts, place a rack in the upper third of the oven and turn the broiler to its highest setting. Preheat for 5 to 10 minutes. Spray a baking sheet with cooking spray.

5 Place 12 phyllo squares on the prepared baking sheet. Top each square with 1 tablespoon of pistachio paste and 1 tablespoon of mini chocolate chips. Squish each marshmallow a bit with your hands and place 1 marshmallow on each s'more. Broil the s'mores until the marshmallows are golden brown on top, about 3 minutes. Keep a close eye on them.

6 Transfer the s'mores to a serving dish and top with the remaining phyllo squares. Serve immediately.

The Various Personalities of

MARSHMALLOW ROASTERS

2

THE TORCH BEARER

is a controversial figure. This person sticks their marshmallow straight into the fire until it catches, then blows it out. This method is repeated until the desired level of char is achieved.

Sweet Potato Pie S'mores

Using a whole sweet potato instead of a sweet potato pie filling here might be controversial, but I think a sweet potato pie should still taste a little like the vegetable! On top of that, the sweet potato and marshmallow are obviously great friends because of the Thanksgiving side dish we all know and love (most of us, anyway!). Here, the sweet potato is coated with sugar and cinnamon and baked to create a caramelized crust. If the sugary tuber is too healthy for you, take the extra mile to grandma's house and use the Sweet Potato Filling (page 56) instead.

Makes 9 🔥 Takes 40 minutes

Nonstick cooking spray

½ cup sugar

1 tablespoon ground cinnamon

Pinch of kosher salt

2 sweet potatoes, peeled and sliced into
   ½-inch-thick rounds

4 tablespoons unsalted butter, melted

2 store-bought refrigerated piecrusts

1½ bars (1.55 ounces each) milk
   chocolate, broken into individual pips

9 regular marshmallows

- -

1 Preheat the oven to 350°F, with a rack in the middle position. Spray 2 baking sheets with cooking spray and set aside.

2 Mix the sugar, cinnamon, and a pinch

of salt in a medium bowl. Set aside.

3 Choose the 9 best sweet potato rounds (store the remaining rounds for another use) and brush them with the

melted butter. Toss them in the sugar mixture to coat. Place the coated sweet potatoes on one of the prepared baking sheets and sprinkle with any remaining sugar.

4 Bake the sweet potatoes, flipping halfway through the baking time, until fork-tender, about 20 minutes. Transfer the baking sheet to a wire rack to cool. Leave the oven on.

5 While the sweet potatoes bake, remove the piecrusts from their packaging and roll them out so they are slightly thinner. Cut each crust into 9 graham cracker–size (2½-inch) squares and place the squares on the remaining prepared baking sheet. Bake the piecrust squares until crispy, about 15 minutes. Transfer 9 baked piecrust squares to a wire rack. Place the

baking sheet with the remaining 9 squares on a heat-proof surface.

6 Using oven mitts, place a rack in the upper third of the oven and turn the broiler to its highest setting. Preheat for 5 to 10 minutes.

7 Top each piecrust square on the baking sheet with 2 chocolate pips and 1 sweet potato round. Squish each marshmallow a bit with your hands and place 1 marshmallow on each sweet potato round. Broil the s'mores until the marshmallows are golden brown on top, about 3 minutes. Keep a close eye on them.

8 Transfer the s'mores to a serving dish and top with the remaining piecrust squares. Serve immediately.

Sweet Potato Filling

4 tablespoons (½ stick) unsalted butter, plus more for greasing the pan
¼ cup granulated sugar
½ cup brown sugar
2 large eggs, lightly beaten
¾ cup evaporated milk
1 tablespoon pure vanilla extract

1 teaspoon ground cinnamon
½ teaspoon ground nutmeg
3 or 4 medium sweet potatoes, peeled, cooked, and mashed (about 2 cups mashed sweet potatoes)
Pinch of kosher salt

1 Preheat the oven to 350°F, with a rack in the middle position. Grease a 9-by-9-inch baking dish with butter. Line it with parchment paper and grease the paper with butter, too.

2 Beat the butter and sugars together in a medium bowl until lightened in color and well combined, about 3 minutes. Add the eggs and beat to combine. Add the milk, vanilla, cinnamon, and nutmeg and stir until combined, 2 minutes.

3 Add the sweet potatoes to the bowl and stir well to combine. Season with a pinch of salt. Pour the mixture into the prepared baking dish.

4 Bake until the pie filling is firm in the center, about 45 minutes. Let it cool on the counter for 30 minutes, then refrigerate, covered, for 2 hours.

5 Cut the cooled pie filling into 2-inch squares and use the squares in place of the sweet potato rounds in Step 7 of the Sweet Potato Pie S'mores recipe.

AS SWEET AS APPLE, ER, S'MORES

Instead of making these pie s'mores from scratch, take a cue from the holiday dinner table. Cut a small square out of leftover pumpkin pie and use it instead of the sweet potato round. But don't stop there! Many other types of pie can be used in this way. Here is a list for inspiration:

Apple	**Coconut Cream**
Banana Cream	**Custard**
Blueberry	**Mississippi Mud**
Buttermilk	**Peanut Butter**
Cherry	**Pecan**
Chess	**Rhubarb**
Chiffon	**Shoofly**

If you want to get crazy, go savory with adaptations inspired by Shepherd's Pie, Chicken Pot Pie, or Thanksgiving Dinner Pie (turkey and cranberries!). Just use scoops of fluffy white potatoes as marshmallows, and drizzle with gravy or pan juices over piecrust squares or buttery crackers and fillings of your choice.

Lemon Meringue
S'mores

emon meringue pie is such a classic dessert, and I love any dessert that is just as tart as it is sweet. Meringue is practically a marshmallow, so this pie is easy to adapt into a s'more. Try it with the alternative filling to make Key Lime Pie s'mores instead! Any leftover curd will keep in the refrigerator in an airtight container for 3 to 4 days. Seal it well and line it with plastic wrap touching the surface of the curd.

Makes 12 🔥 Takes 4 hours

For the lemon curd

½ cup freshly squeezed lemon juice

1 tablespoon lemon zest

½ cup sugar

3 large eggs

6 tablespoons unsalted butter,
    cut into pieces

Pinch of kosher salt

For the s'mores

Nonstick cooking spray

12 regular marshmallows

12 whole graham crackers, broken in half
    to form 24 squares

Confectioners' sugar, for dusting
    (optional)

1   Place the lemon juice, lemon zest, sugar, and eggs in a saucepan over medium heat and whisk together. Add the butter and salt and continue to whisk the mixture until it thickens and coats the back of a spoon, about 5 minutes.

2   Pour the lemon curd into a medium bowl and place a sheet of plastic wrap directly on the surface of the curd. Refrigerate until the curd has firmed up, at least 4 hours.

3 Place a rack in the upper third of the oven and turn the broiler to its highest setting. Preheat for 5 to 10 minutes. Spray a baking sheet with cooking spray.

4 Place the marshmallows on the prepared baking sheet. Broil them until they're golden brown on top, about 3 minutes. Keep a close eye on them.

5 Place 12 graham cracker squares on a serving dish. Top each square with 1 tablespoon of lemon curd, 1 toasted marshmallow, and another graham cracker square. Dust with confectioners' sugar, if using, and serve immediately.

Key Lime Filling

2 tablespoons unsalted butter for
    greasing the pan
2 tablespoons Key lime zest
3 large egg yolks

1 can (14 ounces) sweetened
    condensed milk
½ cup freshly squeezed Key lime juice
Pinch of kosher salt

1 Preheat the oven to 350°F, with a rack in the middle position. Grease a 9-by-9-inch baking dish with butter. Line it with parchment paper and grease the paper with butter, too.

2 Combine the lime zest and egg yolks in a medium bowl. Whisk until the mixture lightens in color and is well combined, 2 minutes.

3 Add the sweetened condensed milk and lime juice. Whisk well to combine.

Season with a pinch of salt. Pour the mixture into the prepared baking dish.

4 Bake until the Key lime filling is set, 15 minutes. Let it cool on the counter for 30 minutes and then refrigerate, covered, for 2 hours.

5 Cut the cooled filling into 2-inch squares and use the squares in place of the lemon curd in Step 5 of the Lemon Meringue S'mores recipe.

Sch'murros

There are a lot of s'mores recipes out there that use an actual churro instead of the graham cracker. As amazing as that may be, I wanted my version to stay true to the s'more stack. Coating the graham crackers in a cinnamon-sugar mixture evokes enough churro flavor without all the effort. However, if you are a churros fanatic and really want to make them from scratch, a recipe for churro rounds follows!

Makes 12 🔥 Takes 15 minutes

Nonstick cooking spray
½ cup sugar
2 tablespoons ground cinnamon
2 tablespoons unsalted butter, melted

12 whole graham crackers, broken in half to form 24 squares
3 bars (1.55 ounces each) milk chocolate, broken into individual pips
12 regular marshmallows

1 Place a rack in the upper third of the oven and turn the broiler to its highest setting. Preheat for 5 to 10 minutes. Spray a baking sheet with cooking spray and set aside.

2 Mix the sugar and cinnamon together in a shallow bowl and set aside.

3 One at a time, brush a very thin coating of melted butter on both sides of a graham cracker square. Immediately dip the cracker into the sugar mixture to coat and set aside on a work surface. Repeat with the remaining graham crackers.

4 Place 12 coated graham cracker squares on the prepared baking sheet. Top each square with 3 chocolate pips. Squish each marshmallow a bit with your hands and place 1 marshmallow on each s'more. Broil until the marshmallows are golden brown on top, about 3 minutes. Keep a close eye on them.

5 Transfer the s'mores to a serving dish and top with the remaining graham cracker squares. Serve immediately.

Homemade Churros

4 cups canola oil or peanut oil

4 tablespoons (½ stick) unsalted butter

½ cup plus 1 tablespoon sugar

¼ teaspoon kosher salt

1 cup water

1 cup all-purpose flour

1 large egg

1½ teaspoons ground cinnamon

1   Heat the oil to 350°F in a fryer, or a large heavy-bottom pot, with a candy thermometer attached (do not let it touch the bottom). Place a wire rack over a drip pan or line a plate with paper towels to soak up any excess frying oil from the finished churros.

2   Place the butter, 1 tablespoon of sugar, and salt in a medium saucepan over medium-high heat and add the water. Bring everything to a simmer.

3   Remove the mixture from the heat and add the flour. Stir well to combine until the dough forms a ball that doesn't stick to the sides of the pan as you stir.

4   Add the egg to the mixture and stir to combine.

5   Meanwhile, pour the cinnamon and the remaining ½ cup of sugar onto a large plate and stir with a fork to combine.

6   Transfer half the dough to a pastry bag fitted with a small star tip (such as a Wilton 1M).

7   Dip a slotted spoon into the hot oil to coat it. Pipe a 1½-inch spiral of churro dough onto the spoon and gently drop it into the hot oil. Fry until lightly golden brown, 2 minutes.

8   Using the slotted spoon, transfer the churro to the prepared rack. Let cool for 1 minute before dredging in the cinnamon sugar. Continue with the remaining dough and cinnamon sugar. Enjoy the finished churros as desired—as is, with coffee, or sandwiched for a s'more.

Tiramisu S'mores

Tiramisu was the first dessert I ever ate at a restaurant. Something about ordering it as a kid when you're going out to eat on your own makes you feel so fancy. Ladyfingers are available at every grocery store and exist (in my opinion) *solely* to make tiramisu. Here, though, I give them a starring role, instead of just letting them be soggy in the center. Any leftover mascarpone filling will keep in an airtight container in the refrigerator for up to 4 days. **Makes 12 🔥 Takes 30 minutes**

12 ounces mascarpone cheese

2 tablespoons sugar

2 individual packets instant coffee
   granules, equivalent to 2 cups
   brewed (I use Starbucks Via packets.)

Nonstick cooking spray

48 ladyfinger cookies

12 regular marshmallows

Cinnamon, for dusting (optional)

1 Stir together the mascarpone, sugar, and coffee granules in a medium bowl, until well combined. Set aside for 10 minutes.

2 Place a rack in the upper third of the oven and turn the broiler to its highest setting. Preheat for 5 to 10 minutes. Spray a baking sheet with cooking spray.

3 Place the ladyfingers in groups of 2 on a serving dish. Spread 1 tablespoon of the mascarpone mixture on the seam between each pair of ladyfingers to fuse them

together. Let sit for 5 minutes while you toast the marshmallows.

4 Place the marshmallows on the prepared baking sheet. Broil them until they're golden brown on top, about 3 minutes. Keep a close eye on them.

5 Place 1 toasted marshmallow on each s'more. Top the s'mores with the remaining ladyfinger pairs and dust with cinnamon, if desired. Serve immediately.

Pancake S'mores

make pancakes at home a lot. This was a last-minute s'more—I was planning to try out a bunch of s'mores ideas that day and had made pancakes for breakfast. Lucky for me, magic happened. The pancakes work perfectly as s'mores crackers because they are nice and soft and you end up not spilling out as much marshmallow as you can with graham crackers. On top of that, the little drizzle of maple syrup really pulls everything together. Bacon is optional, but it gives these s'mores the crunchy element you are missing when using fluffy pancakes instead of graham crackers.

Makes 12 🔥 Takes 30 minutes

1½ cups all-purpose flour
1 tablepoon baking powder
1 teaspoon kosher salt
1 tablespoon sugar
1¼ cups whole milk
1 large egg
4 tablespoons (½ stick) unsalted butter, melted, plus more for greasing the frying pan

1 tablespoon distilled white vinegar
2 bars (1.55 ounces each) milk chocolate, broken into individual pips
Nonstick cooking spray
12 regular marshmallows
6 bacon slices, cooked until crispy and broken into quarters (optional)
½ cup Grade A medium amber maple syrup

1 Mix the flour, baking powder, salt, and sugar in a medium bowl. In another bowl, whisk together the milk, egg, melted butter, and vinegar.

2 Add the liquid ingredients to the dry ingredients and whisk until well combined.

3 Melt a pat of butter in a nonstick frying pan or griddle over medium heat.

4 Working in batches, place 2-tablespoon scoops of pancake batter in the pan to form 2-inch-diameter pancakes. Cook until bubbles pop on the surface and the bottom is golden brown, 2 to 3 minutes. Flip and cook until golden brown, 2 to 3 minutes more. Transfer to a plate and set aside. Continue cooking the remaining batter with more butter, in batches, to make 24 mini pancakes.

5 Place 12 pancakes on a serving dish. Top each pancake with 2 chocolate pips.

6 Place a rack in the upper third of the oven and turn the broiler to its highest setting. Preheat for 5 to 10 minutes. Spray a baking sheet with cooking spray.

7 Place the marshmallows on the prepared baking sheet. Broil them until they're golden brown on top, about 3 minutes. Keep a close eye on them.

8 Place 1 toasted marshmallow on each s'more, followed by 2 pieces of bacon, if using. Drizzle 2 teaspoons of maple syrup over each s'more. Top the s'mores with the remaining pancakes. Serve immediately.

A NEW KIND OF BREAKFAST STACK

You've heard of breakfast for dinner . . . but have you heard of s'mores for breakfast? If not, it's time to add this concept to your repertoire. Because so many morning meals are just an excuse to serve up some sugar, why not create a whole spread with s'mores riffs to inspire innovative stacks of breakfast foods? Serve this bountiful breakfast buffet with orange juice, coffee, and hot chocolate with marshmallows (plus a graham cracker stick stirrer for extra charm), of course.

Here are a few s'mores breakfast components to mix and match (bonus points for extra-crazy combinations):

Crunchy: toasted English muffins, baked oatmeal cut into squares, mini waffles, biscuits, hash brown squares, toast, granola bars, graham crackers, crispy bacon strips

Gooey: poached eggs, yogurt, marshmallows (especially the spreadable version!), avocado, cottage cheese, bananas, peanut or other nut butters, cream cheese

Melty: hollandaise, pesto, fruit jams and jellies, Nutella, hot honey, cheese, spicy tomato sauce

Rocky Road
S'mores

Rocky road ice cream is pretty much just s'mores ingredients with almonds added, so it would be wrong not to include a rocky road s'more in a roundup of s'mores riffs. I experimented with chocolate-covered almonds, almond candy bark, and a few other variations (hard work, but someone had to do it), and liked the results best when just topping the chocolate with roasted almonds. If you'd prefer less crunch from the almonds, chop or crush them before topping the s'mores in Step 3. **Makes 12 🔥 Takes 10 minutes**

Nonstick cooking spray

12 whole graham crackers, broken in half
  to form 24 squares

3 bars (1.55 ounces each) milk chocolate,
  broken into individual pips

84 roasted, lightly salted almonds

12 regular marshmallows

1 Place a rack in the upper third of the oven and turn the broiler to its highest setting. Preheat for 5 to 10 minutes. Spray a baking sheet with cooking spray.

2 Place 12 graham cracker squares on the prepared baking sheet. Top each square with 3 chocolate pips. Broil just to soften the chocolate slightly, about 30 seconds.

3 Remove from the broiler and top each s'more with 7 roasted almonds. Squish each marshmallow a bit with your hands and place 1 marshmallow on each s'more. Broil the s'mores until the marshmallows are golden brown on top, about 3 minutes. Keep a close eye on them.

4 Transfer the s'mores to a serving dish and top with the remaining graham cracker squares. Serve immediately.

Cheesecake S'mores

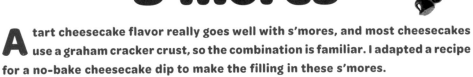

A tart cheesecake flavor really goes well with s'mores, and most cheesecakes use a graham cracker crust, so the combination is familiar. I adapted a recipe for a no-bake cheesecake dip to make the filling in these s'mores.

Makes 12 🔥 Takes 20 minutes

1 cup cream cheese (from a tub,
   not a brick)
¼ cup confectioners' sugar
¼ teaspoon pure vanilla extract
Nonstick cooking spray

12 regular marshmallows
12 whole graham crackers, broken in half
   to form 24 squares
¾ cup mini chocolate chips

1 Mix the cream cheese, confectioners' sugar, and vanilla in a medium bowl. Cover the bowl and refrigerate until needed.

2 Place a rack in the upper third of the oven and turn the broiler to its highest setting. Preheat for 5 to 10 minutes. Spray a baking sheet with cooking spray.

3 Place the marshmallows on the prepared baking sheet. Broil them until they're golden brown on top, about 3 minutes. Keep a close eye on them.

4 Place 12 graham cracker squares on a serving dish. Top each square with 1 heaping tablespoon of the cheesecake mixture, followed by 1 tablespoon of the mini chocolate chips.

5 Place 1 toasted marshmallow on each s'more. Top the s'mores with the remaining graham cracker squares. Serve immediately.

Gimme S'moreos

I have a philosophy when I am mashing up recipes—if the names of the two dishes can seamlessly be combined, you know you are heading in the right direction. These S'moreos are the perfect example. **Makes 12 ☘ Takes 10 minutes**

Nonstick cooking spray
24 crème-filled chocolate sandwich
   cookies

2 bars (1.55 ounces each) milk chocolate,
   broken into individual pips
12 regular marshmallows

1 Place a rack in the upper third of the oven and turn the broiler to its highest setting. Preheat for 5 to 10 minutes. Spray a baking sheet with cooking spray.

2 Place 12 sandwich cookies on the prepared baking sheet. Top each cookie with 2 chocolate pips. Squish each marshmallow a bit with your hands and

place 1 marshmallow on each s'more. Broil the s'mores until the marshmallows are golden brown on top, about 3 minutes. Keep a close eye on them.

3 Transfer the s'mores to a serving dish and top with the remaining cookies. Serve immediately.

More Sweet and Savory Substitutions for Graham Crackers

Biscuits

Brioche

Chocolate chip cookies

Cornbread

Cream puffs or eclairs, halved lengthwise

Croissants

Dense cake slices

Egg matzo

Fudge Stripes

Milano cookies

Naan

Nutter Butters

Oatmeal raisin cookies

Peanut butter cookies

Ritz crackers

Shortbread cookies

Snickerdoodles

Spiced molasses cookies

Sticky buns

Sugar cookies

Sugar wafers

Thin brownies

Vanilla wafers

Wheat Thins

Pizzelle S'mores

I have my grandmother's pizzelle maker, and her recipe for these delicate anise-flavored vanilla cookies is written in permanent marker right on the side of the box. It's great because I never need to go searching for a pizzelle recipe—I just take out the machine and go. If you are similarly blessed with an heirloom pizzelle iron, you must try this recipe ASAP. Pizzelles are a great graham cracker replacement, and if you squeeze these s'mores tightly closed, you can almost serve them as cookies. If you don't have the requisite equipment, I urge you to consider making room for it in your home and your heart. In a pinch, though, you should be able to find suitable pizzelles in the cookie or bakery aisle of your grocery store. **Makes 12 🔥 Takes 40 minutes**

For the pizzelles
1¾ cups sifted all-purpose flour
¾ cup sugar
2 teaspoons baking powder
½ teaspoon kosher salt
3 large eggs
8 tablespoons (1 stick) unsalted butter, melted
¼ teaspoon anise extract
1 teaspoon pure vanilla extract
Nonstick cooking spray

For the s'mores filling
1 cup semisweet chocolate chips
¼ cup heavy (whipping) cream
Pinch of kosher salt
12 regular marshmallows

1   Mix the flour, sugar, baking powder, and salt in a large bowl.

2   Crack the eggs into another large bowl and add the melted butter, anise extract, and vanilla, whisking to combine. Add the egg mixture to the flour mixture and stir well to combine.

3   Preheat the pizzelle iron according to the manufacturer's instructions and grease it with cooking spray.

4   While the iron preheats, make the ganache. Combine the chocolate chips, cream, and salt in a small microwave-safe bowl. Microwave on medium power for 30-second intervals, stirring after each interval, until the chocolate is just melted and the mixture is combined. Be careful not to overheat the ganache, as it can become grainy. Set aside.

5   When the iron is hot, scoop 2 teaspoons of batter into the middle of each space (or slightly toward the hinge) on your iron. Close the iron and cook for about 30 seconds, depending on how hot your iron gets. Use a thin spatula to transfer the pizzelles to a wire rack or work surface. Repeat with the remaining batter until you have 24 pizzelles.

6   Spread about 2 teaspoons of ganache on one side of each pizzelle.

7   Place a rack in the upper third of the oven and turn the broiler to its highest setting. Preheat for 5 to 10 minutes. Spray a baking sheet with cooking spray.

8   Place the marshmallows on the prepared baking sheet. Broil them until they're golden brown on top, about 3 minutes. Keep a close eye on them.

9   Place 1 toasted marshmallow on each s'more. Top the s'mores with the remaining pizzelles, pressing down to flatten the s'mores a bit. Transfer to a serving dish. Serve immediately.

Cannoli
S'mores

When you think of cannoli, you might imagine a cylindrical flute of crunchy goodness with a creamy ricotta interior. Well, it's time to rethink that shape! Enter the cannoli stack. Making a square cannoli shell is not nearly as hard as making a tube. Any leftover ricotta can be stored in an airtight container in the refrigerator for up to 4 days. **Makes 12 🔥 Takes 30 minutes**

2 cups all-purpose flour, plus more
    for the work surface
2 tablespoons cold shortening (put it in
    the fridge for at least 1 hour before
    you need to use it)
1 teaspoon granulated sugar
½ cup dry white wine
1 cup canola oil or peanut oil

1 cup whole-milk ricotta cheese
¼ cup confectioners' sugar
¼ teaspoon pure vanilla extract
¼ teaspoon ground cinnamon
Nonstick cooking spray
¾ cup mini chocolate chips
12 regular marshmallows

1   Place the flour and shortening in a medium bowl. Using a fork, cut the shortening into the flour until you see pea-size pieces of shortening. Stir in the granulated sugar. One tablespoon at a time, stir in the wine until the dough

comes together. Mix well. The dough should be very thick, like pasta dough.

2   Dust a clean work surface with flour and transfer the dough to it. Using a rolling pin, roll it out until it's very thin, about ⅛ inch thick and roughly 10 by 15 inches. Cut the dough into 24 graham cracker–size (2½-inch) squares.

3 Heat about ½ inch of the oil to 375°F in a deep skillet or 12-inch pot over medium-high heat with a candy thermometer attached (do not let it touch the bottom). Place a wire rack over a drip pan or line a plate with paper towels. If you don't have a candy thermometer, test the oil by adding a scrap of the dough to the oil. If it bubbles up immediately, the oil is ready.

4 Working in batches if needed, carefully add the cannoli squares to the hot oil. Fry until the dough bubbles up and becomes crispy, about 20 seconds per side. Use tongs to remove the cannoli squares from the oil and transfer them to the prepared rack or plate to drain.

5 Place the ricotta, confectioners' sugar, vanilla, and cinnamon into a medium bowl and stir until combined. Cover the bowl and refrigerate until needed.

6 Place a rack in the upper third of the oven and turn the broiler to its highest setting. Preheat for 5 to 10 minutes. Spray a baking sheet with cooking spray.

7 Place the marshmallows on the prepared baking sheet. Broil them until they're golden brown on top, about 3 minutes. Keep a close eye on them.

8 Transfer 12 cannoli squares to a serving dish. Top each square with 1 heaping tablespoon of the ricotta mixture and 1 tablespoon of mini chocolate chips.

9 Place 1 toasted marshmallow on each s'more. Top the s'mores with the remaining cannoli squares. Serve immediately.

The Various Personalities of
MARSHMALLOW ROASTERS

3

THE MULTI-TASKER

usually has a stick in each hand and several marshmallows on each stick. They are making a few for themselves because they want one s'more and at least one marshmallow on its own (they love that "pure" taste). These overachievers are also toasting some for a few people they offered to help.

Tiny S'mores

The number one rule on the internet (and in life) is tiny things are always cuter than their normal-size counterparts. These baby s'mores are no exception. They are easier to make than you would expect and are extremely poppable. For added fun, you feel like a giant while you eat them. If you're a chocolate lover, up the chip count to 48 and place one chip on each square of cereal. Having chocolate on both sides of the mallow also acts as a great adhesive. **Makes 24 🔥 Takes 15 minutes**

Nonstick cooking spray
48 pieces of small square cereal
(Golden Grahams or Cinnamon Toast
Crunch work well)

24 (regular-size) milk chocolate chips
24 mini marshmallows

1   Place a rack in the upper third of the oven and turn the broiler to its highest setting. Preheat for 5 to 10 minutes. Spray a baking sheet with cooking spray.

2   Line up 24 pieces of cereal on a baking sheet. Top each piece of cereal with 1 piece of chocolate. Broil until the chocolate softens, about 1 minute.

3   Remove the baking sheet from the oven and place 1 marshmallow on each tiny s'more—the softened chocolate will help it stick. Return the baking sheet to the oven and broil until the marshmallows are browned, about 3 minutes. Keep a close eye on them.

4   Remove the baking sheet from the oven and place the 24 remaining cereal pieces on top of the marshmallows to form mini s'mores. Transfer the mini s'mores to a serving dish. Serve immediately.

Huge S'mores

You knew if there were Tiny S'mores (page 83), there would be big ones, too. I use regular marshmallows for this, but if you want to go jumbo, you can find the large variety in certain grocery stores, or buy them online. No such luck with the large graham crackers, though. You need to make them yourself! **Makes 1 🔥 Takes 2 hours**

All-purpose flour, for dusting the work surface
Dough from 1 batch Homemade Honey Graham Crackers (page 15)

Nonstick cooking spray
4 bars (1.55 ounces each) milk chocolate, broken into individual pips
16 regular marshmallows

1 Preheat the oven to 350°F. Line two baking sheets with parchment paper.

2 Lightly flour a work surface and place the dough on it. Using a rolling pin, roll out the dough to about a ⅛-inch thickness. Cut the dough into two 8-inch squares. Carefully transfer the squares to the prepared baking sheets. Bake until golden brown and slightly firm to the touch, about 15 minutes. Let cool for at least 15 minutes before using.

3 Using oven mitts, place a rack in the upper third of the oven and turn the broiler to its highest setting. Preheat for 5 to 10 minutes. Spray another baking sheet with cooking spray.

4 Place 1 graham cracker square on the prepared baking sheet and cover it with all of the chocolate. Squish the marshmallows a bit with your hands and line them up on the chocolate. Broil the s'more until golden brown, 3 to 5 minutes. Keep a close eye on it.

5 Transfer the s'more to a serving dish and top with the remaining graham cracker square. Serve immediately.

WORLD RECORD S'MORES

According to Guinness World Records, the largest s'more weighed in at 267 pounds and was made at the Deer Run Camping Resort in Gardners, Pennsylvania, on May 31, 2014. A total of 104 volunteers worked together to make the s'more. However, pastry chef Jennie Strong and pastry lead Audrey Clous believe they beat that record when on Sunday, October 9, 2017, they made a s'more at Jackson Lake Lodge in Grand Teton National Park, Wyoming, weighing in at 440 pounds. Their attempt remains to be verified by Guinness World Records.

Strawberry Shmortcakes

Strawberry shortcake is one of those desserts I never think to make, but when I eat it, I'm reminded how much I love it. It was something we had a lot growing up, and it always tastes a little bit like home. Using shortbread cookies instead of graham crackers really drives home the strawberry shortcake flavor!

Makes 12 ⚲ Takes 10 minutes, plus 1 hour to rest

6 large fresh strawberries, hulled
   and halved top to bottom
1 tablespoon sugar
Pinch of kosher salt
Nonstick cooking spray

24 shortbread cookies
1 bar (1.55 ounces) milk chocolate,
   broken into individual pips
12 regular marshmallows

1 Place the strawberry halves into a small bowl. Add the sugar and salt and gently stir to combine. Cover and refrigerate for 1 hour to macerate.

2 Place a rack in the upper third of the oven and turn the broiler to its highest setting. Preheat for 5 to 10 minutes. Spray a baking sheet with cooking spray.

3 Place 12 shortbread cookies on the prepared baking sheet. Top each cookie with 1 chocolate pip. Squish each marshmallow a bit with your hands and place 1 marshmallow on each pip. Broil the s'mores until the marshmallows are golden brown on top, about 3 minutes. Keep a close eye on them.

4 Transfer the s'mores to a serving dish. Top each marshmallow with a strawberry half and another cookie. Serve immediately.

Black Forest S'mores

Dark cherries and chocolate are a match for the ages. I like making a compote to give these s'mores that deep cherry punch. Any leftover cherry compote will keep in an airtight container in the refrigerator for up to 4 days. **Makes 12 🔥 Takes 30 minutes**

36 sweet cherries, stemmed, pitted, and
    chopped
¼ cup freshly squeezed orange juice
2 tablespoons sugar
Pinch of kosher salt
1 teaspoon cornstarch
2 tablespoons water

Nonstick cooking spray
12 whole chocolate graham crackers,
    broken in half to form 24 squares
3 bars (1.55 ounces each) milk chocolate,
    broken into individual pips
12 regular marshmallows

1   Place the cherries, orange juice, sugar, and salt in a saucepan over medium high heat and bring to a simmer. Reduce the heat to low and cook for 15 minutes.

2   Whisk the cornstarch with the water in a small bowl, until combined, and add it to the cherry mixture. Simmer until thickened, 5 minutes more.

3   Place a rack in the upper third of the oven and turn the broiler to its highest setting. Preheat for 5 to 10 minutes. Spray a baking sheet with cooking spray.

4   Place 12 graham cracker squares on the prepared baking sheet. Top each square with 3 chocolate pips. Broil just to soften the chocolate slightly, about 30 seconds.

5   Squish each marshmallow a bit with your hands and place 1 marshmallow on each s'more. Broil the s'mores until the marshmallows are golden brown on top, about 3 minutes. Keep a close eye on them.

6   Transfer the s'mores to a serving dish. Top each marshmallow with a spoonful of the cherry mixture and another graham cracker square. Serve immediately.

Potato Chip S'mores

Putting marshmallow and chocolate on a potato chip is just unusual enough to be surprising, but once you've tried it, the combination seems so obvious. These need ganache instead of the typical chocolate bar to adapt to the shape of the potato chip. Once you squeeze the melted chocolate and creamy marshmallow between two crunchy chips, you may not be able to go back to grahams. **Makes 12** 🔥 **Takes 20 minutes**

½ cup semisweet chocolate chips
2 tablespoons heavy (whipping) cream
Pinch of kosher salt

Nonstick cooking spray
12 regular marshmallows
24 crinkle-cut wavy potato chips

1 Combine the chocolate chips, cream, and salt in a small microwave-safe bowl. Microwave on medium power for 15-second intervals, stirring after each interval, until the chocolate is just melted and the mixture is combined. Be careful not to overheat the ganache, as it can become grainy.

2 Place a rack in the upper third of the oven and turn the broiler to its highest setting. Preheat for 5 to 10 minutes. Spray a baking sheet with cooking spray.

3 Place 12 chips on a serving dish. Top each chip with 1 teaspoon of ganache. (You should have just enough for all the chips.)

4 Place the marshmallows on the prepared baking sheet. Broil them until they're golden brown on top, about 3 minutes. Keep a close eye on them.

5 Place 1 toasted marshmallow on each s'more. Top the s'mores with the remaining chips. Serve immediately.

Pretzel S'mores

Adding pretzels to a s'more adds so much dimension to the sweet sandwich that you may start looking for something salty in every s'more you make! Don't say I didn't warn you. If you didn't get enough pretzel and want to go full-on savory with this recipe, substitute pretzel chips for the graham cracker squares (and omit the interior pretzel). If you really want to get into it, use a long pretzel stick to toast your marshmallow. **Makes 12 🔥 Takes 10 minutes**

Nonstick cooking spray

12 whole graham crackers, broken in half to form 24 squares

3 bars (1.55 ounces each) milk chocolate, broken into individual pips

36 pretzels

12 regular marshmallows

1 Place a rack in the upper third of the oven and turn the broiler to its highest setting. Preheat for 5 to 10 minutes. Spray a baking sheet with cooking spray.

2 Place 12 graham cracker squares on the prepared baking sheet. Top each square with 3 chocolate pips. Broil just to soften the chocolate slightly, about 30 seconds.

3 Top each s'more with 3 pretzels. Squish each marshmallow a bit with your hands and place 1 marshmallow on each s'more. Broil again until the marshmallows are golden brown on top, about 3 minutes. Keep a close eye on them.

4 Transfer the s'mores to a serving dish and top with the remaining graham cracker squares. Serve immediately.

Caramel Corn
S'mores

Popcorn is so underrated in desserts! Using kettle corn and a little caramel in this s'more gives it such a classic take-me-out-to-the-ball-game flavor.

Makes 12 ⚲ Takes 15 minutes

Nonstick cooking spray

12 whole graham crackers, broken in half to form 24 squares

¾ cup Salted Caramel Sauce (page 29)

1 overflowing cup popped kettle corn

12 regular marshmallows

1   Place a rack in the upper third of the oven and turn the broiler to its highest setting. Preheat for 5 to 10 minutes. Spray a baking sheet with cooking spray.

2   Place 12 graham cracker squares on the prepared baking sheet. Drizzle each square with 1½ teaspoons of salted caramel sauce and top each with about 7 popcorn kernels. Drizzle the popcorn with another

1½ teaspoons of salted caramel. Squish each marshmallow a bit with your hands and place 1 marshmallow on each s'more. Broil the s'mores until the marshmallows are golden brown on top, about 3 minutes. Keep a close eye on them.

3   Transfer the s'mores to a serving dish and top with the remaining graham cracker squares. Serve immediately.

Olive Oil and Balsamic S'mores

I sometimes like to put oil and vinegar on my ice cream, and the combination translated to s'mores easily. The oil adds a richness to the s'more and the vinegar cuts the sweetness. Since for me, salt is always welcome in a dessert, I've added a finishing sprinkle of sea salt as well. Make sure to grab a thick balsamic syrup to add that extra oomph. **Makes 12 🔥 Takes 15 minutes**

Nonstick cooking spray

12 whole graham crackers, broken in half to form 24 squares

2 bars (1.55 ounces each) milk chocolate, broken into individual pips

12 regular marshmallows

¼ cup extra-virgin olive oil

¼ cup balsamic syrup

1 tablespoon flaky sea salt

1 Place a rack in the upper third of the oven and turn the broiler to its highest setting. Preheat for 5 to 10 minutes. Spray a baking sheet with cooking spray.

2 Place 12 graham cracker squares on the prepared baking sheet. Top each square with 2 chocolate pips. Squish each marshmallow a bit with your hands and place 1 marshmallow on each s'more.

Broil the s'mores until the marshmallows are golden brown on top, about 3 minutes. Keep a close eye on them.

3 Transfer the s'mores to a serving dish. Evenly drizzle the oil and then the balsamic syrup over the marshmallows. Sprinkle with sea salt and top the s'mores with the remaining graham cracker squares. Serve immediately.

How a Marshmallow Is Made

How do store-bought marshmallows become so uniform and rounded in shape? Marshmallow manufacturers boil the sweeteners and dissolve the gelatin in water, then combine the two. The mixture is then heated to around 240°F and strained. After straining, an intense amount of air is blasted through the mixture to give it its signature puffiness. A process known as *extrusion* squeezes the puffs through tubes, forming long ropes that are dusted with cornstarch to prevent sticking and help maintain their shape, and finally cut into your typical marshmallow sizes.

Bacon S'mores

Chocolate-covered bacon was all the rage on the internet a few years back. As I do with any trend, I stepped back to think: *After all the hype is over, what else can this become?* The answer? The crunchy cracker of a s'more! You can add graham crackers to this recipe, if you want, but I like the pure simplicity of the bacon, chocolate, and marshmallow. **Makes 12 ♨ Takes 30 minutes**

24 bacon slices
1 cup semisweet chocolate chips
¼ cup heavy (whipping) cream

Pinch of kosher salt
Nonstick cooking spray
12 regular marshmallows

1   To magically transform your bacon into a cracker shape, cut each strip in half and press the fatty parts together to form a square. Place the squares in a skillet over medium heat (you may need to work in batches) and use a spatula or a steak weight to press the bacon down as it cooks and fuses into a glassy pane, 3 to 4 minutes per side.

2   Combine the chocolate chips, cream, and salt in a microwave-safe bowl. Microwave on medium power for 30-second intervals, stirring after each interval, until the chocolate is just melted and the mixture is combined. Be careful not to overheat the ganache, as it can become grainy.

3   Place a rack in the upper third of the oven and turn the broiler to its highest setting. Preheat for 5 to 10 minutes. Spray a baking sheet with cooking spray.

4   Place the marshmallows on the prepared baking sheet. Broil them until they're golden brown on top, about 3 minutes. Keep a close eye on them.

5   Transfer 12 bacon squares to a serving dish. Top each square with 2 teaspoons of ganache, 1 toasted marshmallow, and another square of bacon. Serve immediately.

Mexican Chocolate S'mores

I crave that slight smoky flavor of Mexican chocolate, and to approximate it, I have introduced heat and cinnamon to this s'more. It works perfectly. As simple as it seems, adding a spice blend to a classic s'more changes everything.

Makes 12 🔥 Takes 10 minutes

Nonstick cooking spray

12 whole graham crackers, broken in half to form 24 squares

3 bars (1.55 ounces each) milk chocolate, broken into individual pips

2 tablespoons crushed red pepper flakes

1 tablespoon ground cinnamon

12 regular marshmallows

. . . .

1 Place a rack in the upper third of the oven and turn the broiler to its highest setting. Preheat for 5 to 10 minutes. Spray a baking sheet with cooking spray.

2 Place 12 graham cracker squares on the prepared baking sheet. Top each square with 3 chocolate pips. Broil just to soften the chocolate slightly, about 30 seconds.

3 Sprinkle ½ teaspoon of crushed red pepper flakes and a pinch of cinnamon on top of the softened chocolate on each s'more. Squish each marshmallow a bit with your hands and place 1 marshmallow on each s'more. Broil the s'mores until the marshmallows are golden brown on top, about 3 minutes. Keep a close eye on them.

4 Transfer the s'mores to a serving dish and top with the remaining graham cracker squares. Serve immediately.

Elvis S'mores

You have to give it to the King—the rich, nutty, and sweet flavor combo of peanut butter, banana, and bacon is amazing. These ingredients come together in a few awesome "I can't help falling in love with you" bites. **Makes 12 🔥 Takes 15 minutes**

Nonstick cooking spray

12 whole graham crackers, broken in half to form 24 squares

1 cup creamy peanut butter

2 very ripe bananas, each cut into 12 pieces

6 bacon slices, cooked until crispy and broken in half widthwise

12 regular marshmallows

. . . .

1　Place a rack in the upper third of the oven and turn the broiler to its highest setting. Preheat for 5 to 10 minutes. Spray a baking sheet with cooking spray.

2　Place 12 graham cracker squares on the prepared baking sheet. Spread about 1 heaping tablespoon of peanut butter on each square. Top each square with 2 banana slices and 1 piece of bacon.

Squish each marshmallow a bit with your hands and place 1 marshmallow on each piece of bacon. Broil the s'mores until the marshmallows are golden brown on top, about 3 minutes. Keep a close eye on them.

3　Transfer the s'mores to a serving dish and top with the remaining graham cracker squares. Serve immediately.

THE KING OF CURIOUS COMBOS

Elvis Presley was renowned for his strange cravings and culinary tastes, but his namesake peanut butter, banana, and bacon sandwich is just the tip of the iceberg. He discovered it on February 1, 1976, when he flew from Graceland to Denver and back in one night for the sole purpose of eating a Fool's Gold Loaf—a $50 sandwich made at the Colorado Mine Company (his favorite local restaurant). The 8,000 calorie sandwich consisted of a hollowed-out loaf of bread filled with a jar's worth of peanut butter, a jar's worth of grape jelly, and a pound of bacon. Elvis's other favorite dishes included barbecued bologna, meatballs wrapped in bacon, and tomato fritters.

Jalapeño Jam S'mores

You can probably tell by now that I love a good sweet-spicy combo! This recipe makes a lot of extra jam because of the size of the pectin packages. Jalapeño jam will keep well in your fridge in an airtight container for up to a month. Serve it with a bagel, on toast, or, of course, on this s'more!

Makes 12 🔥 Takes 40 minutes, plus an overnight rest

15 jalapeño peppers, stemmed

1 red bell pepper, stemmed, seeded, and finely diced

4 cups sugar

1½ cups apple cider vinegar

Pinch of kosher salt

1 box (1.75 ounces) pectin

12 whole graham crackers, broken in half to form 24 squares

3 bars (1.55 ounces each) milk chocolate, broken into individual pips

12 regular marshmallows

1 Remove about half the seeds from the jalapeños (remove them all if you don't want any heat). Finely dice the jalapeños and place them in a saucepan. Add the red bell pepper, sugar, vinegar, and salt. Place the pan over medium heat. Cook until the peppers are softened, the sugar is melted, and the jam has a syrupy consistency, 15 minutes.

2 Stir in the pectin. Simmer for 1 minute more. Pour the jam into 2 pint-size Mason jars to cool. Cover the jars and refrigerate the jam overnight before using.

3 Place a rack in the upper third of the oven and turn the broiler to its highest setting. Preheat for 5 to 10 minutes. Spray a baking sheet with cooking spray.

4 Place 12 graham cracker squares on the prepared baking sheet. Top each square with 3 chocolate pips. Squish each marshmallow a bit with your hands and place 1 marshmallow on each s'more. Broil the s'mores until the marshmallows are golden brown on top, about 3 minutes. Keep a close eye on them.

5 Transfer the s'mores to a serving dish. Drizzle 1 tablespoon of jalapeño jam on each marshmallow and top with another graham cracker square. Serve immediately.

Other Jams

A humorous playlist for a s'mores-inspired gathering, including old and new classics, and—where applicable—the stack (or ingredient) to pair them with:

Campfire classic
"This Land Is Your Land"
—pair with apple butter

Bob Dylan
"Blowin' in the Wind"

Gram "Graham" Parsons
"Love Hurts"

Elvis
"Burning Love"
—pair with Elvis S'mores (page 100)

Britney Spears
". . . Baby One S'more Time"

Campfire classic
"Baby Bumble Bee"
—pair with fig and honey jam

Jimi Hendrix
"Fire"

Campfire classic
"Down by the Bay"
—pair with watermelon jelly

Campfire classic
"Kookaburra Sits in the Old Gum Tree"
—pair with vegemite

Selena Gomez, Marshmello
"Wolves"

The 1975
"Chocolate"

Campfire classic
"Home on the Range"
—pair with peach habanero jelly

DRAM and Neil Young
"Campfire"

Busta Rhymes
"Gimme S'more"

Campfire classic
"Apples and Bananas"
—pair with Berry Banana S'mores (page 32) or Caramel Apple S'mores (page 43)

The Beatles
"Strawberry Fields Forever"
—pair with strawberry rhubarb jam

Chile Mango S'mores

At a local juicery, I love buying the mango coated with chile powder. I know it's a waste when I could easily just make it myself, but it's so convenient and delicious! I crave the sweet and spicy combo, and I can't pass it by when I see it. One day I realized that this would be perfect in a s'more—and I made it immediately!

Makes 12 🔥 **Takes 15 minutes**

Nonstick cooking spray

12 whole graham crackers, broken in half to form 24 squares

3 bars (1.55 ounces each) milk chocolate, broken into individual pips

2 ripe mangos, peeled, pitted, and cut into 36 slices

2 tablespoons crushed red pepper flakes

12 regular marshmallows

. . . .

1 Place a rack in the upper third of the oven and turn the broiler to its highest setting. Preheat for 5 to 10 minutes. Spray a baking sheet with cooking spray.

2 Place 12 graham cracker squares on the prepared baking sheet. Top each square with 3 chocolate pips. Broil just to soften the chocolate slightly, about 30 seconds.

3 Add about 3 mango slices to each s'more. Sprinkle ½ teaspoon of crushed red pepper flakes on top of the mango. Squish each marshmallow a bit with your hands and place 1 marshmallow on each s'more. Broil the s'mores until the marshmallows are golden brown on top, about 3 minutes. Keep a close eye on them.

4 Transfer the s'mores to a serving dish and top with the remaining graham cracker squares. Serve immediately.

Hot Snickers S'mores

The combo of caramel, sriracha, and peanut in this s'more is almost like a Snickers bar, but with a spicy twist. Sriracha works well in sweet applications, particularly when paired with other savory ingredients—in this case, peanuts.

Makes 12 🏕 Takes 30 minutes

¾ cup Salted Caramel Sauce (page 29)

¼ cup sriracha

Nonstick cooking spray

12 whole graham crackers, broken in half to form 24 squares

3 bars (1.55 ounces each) milk chocolate, broken into individual pips

1 cup roasted salted peanuts

12 regular marshmallows

1   Place the salted caramel sauce in a small bowl and add the sriracha. Stir to combine.

2   Place a rack in the upper third of the oven and turn the broiler to its highest setting. Preheat for 5 to 10 minutes. Spray a baking sheet with cooking spray.

3   Place 12 graham cracker squares on the prepared baking sheet. Top each square with 3 chocolate pips. Drizzle with 1½ teaspoons of sriracha caramel sauce and top each with about 10 peanuts. Drizzle another 1½ teaspoons of caramel over the peanuts. Squish each marshmallow a bit with your hands and place 1 marshmallow on each s'more. Broil the s'mores until the marshmallows are golden brown on top, about 3 minutes. Keep a close eye on them.

4   Transfer the s'mores to a serving dish and top with the remaining graham cracker squares. Serve immediately.

The Various Personalities of
MARSHMALLOW ROASTERS

4

No campfire would be complete without the **FIRE SAFETY SCOUT**. This well-meaning person will tell you not to eat your marshmallow when it's too hot (you'll burn your mouth!). They will tell you not to put your hands so close to the fire while roasting, or your feet so close to the fire while eating. And they will inform you that eating a burned marshmallow can cause cancer.

Grilled Peach and Basil S'mores

Grilling peaches really brings out the sweetness in the fruit and boosts the charred flavors you expect in s'mores. I like to pair peaches with basil, and firmly believe that basil should be included in more desserts. **Makes 12 ⚸ Takes 20 minutes**

Nonstick cooking spray

2 peaches, halved and pitted

1 tablespoon extra-virgin olive oil

½ teaspoon kosher salt

12 whole graham crackers, broken in half
  to form 24 squares

2 bars (1.55 ounces each) milk chocolate,
  broken into individual pips

12 regular marshmallows

12 fresh basil leaves

- -

1　Heat a grill to high or place a grill pan over high heat. Place a rack in the upper third of the oven and turn the broiler to its highest setting. Preheat for 5 to 10 minutes. Spray a baking sheet with cooking spray.

2　Place the peach halves in a medium bowl with the olive oil and salt and toss to coat. Grill them until they're brown and charred with grill marks, about 5 minutes. Flip and grill the other side, 5 minutes more. Transfer the peaches to a plate. When they're cool, slice each peach half into 6 wedges.

3　Place 12 graham cracker squares on the prepared baking sheet. Top each square with 2 chocolate pips and then 2 peach wedges. Squish each marshmallow a bit with your hands and place 1 marshmallow on each s'more. Broil until the marshmallows are golden brown on top, about 3 minutes. Keep a close eye on them.

4　Transfer the s'mores to a serving dish. Top each marshmallow with 1 basil leaf and another graham cracker square. Serve immediately.

Pear and Candied Ginger S'mores

Pears are naturally so sweet—I personally think they need something to balance all that cloying flavor. In this s'more, the sharp, spicy ginger and dark chocolate do that job. **Makes 12 🔥 Takes 15 minutes**

Nonstick cooking spray

12 whole graham crackers, broken in half to form 24 squares

3 bars (1.55 ounces each) dark chocolate, broken into individual pips

2 ripe pears, thinly sliced (I use Bosc.)

¾ cup chopped candied ginger

12 regular marshmallows

. . . .

1   Place a rack in the upper third of the oven and turn the broiler to its highest setting. Preheat for 5 to 10 minutes. Spray a baking sheet with cooking spray.

2   Place 12 graham cracker squares on the prepared baking sheet. Top each square with 3 chocolate pips. Broil just to soften the chocolate slightly, about 30 seconds.

3   Add 3 or 4 pear slices to each s'more and sprinkle each with 1 tablespoon of chopped candied ginger. Squish each marshmallow a bit with your hands and place 1 marshmallow on each s'more. Broil the s'mores until the marshmallows are golden brown on top, about 3 minutes. Keep a close eye on them.

4   Transfer the s'mores to a serving dish and top with the remaining graham cracker squares. Serve immediately.

PLAYING WITH FIRE

Simon Turner, a daredevil New Zealander, made news when he roasted a marshmallow over a lava lake in the Marcum Crater, a volcanic vent in Oceania. As the US Geological Survey warned over Twitter in 2018, not only is this practice unsafe—sulfuric acid plus sugar equals an exothermic reaction—but your marshmallow would, best case, taste very bad, or, worst case, poison you.

If you, too, want to make some bad decisions while toasting a marshmallow, there are certainly enough household items (candles, heating grate, curling iron, hair dryer, doggie breath, and so on) that might intrigue the curious pyromaniac. Given the history of poor choices when it comes to household appliances and food items (such as the famous clothes-iron grilled-cheese press), we recommend that you keep this party around flames that are meant for cooking.

Everything Bagel
S'mores

Everything is a bit of a misleading title for this s'more because I kept the onion and garlic out of the spice mixture. To me, the cream cheese, sesame seeds, and poppy seeds are enough to evoke an everything bagel flavor—onion and garlic don't really have a place in dessert. If you want to up the bagel (and savory) ante, use bagel chips instead of the graham cracker squares. **Makes 12 🔥 Takes 15 minutes**

Nonstick cooking spray

12 whole graham crackers, broken in half
    to form 24 squares

1 cup cream cheese
    (from a tub, not a brick)

2 tablespoons sesame seeds

2 tablespoons poppy seeds

12 regular marshmallows

1 Place a rack in the upper third of the oven and turn the broiler to its highest setting. Preheat for 5 to 10 minutes. Spray a baking sheet with cooking spray.

2 Place 12 graham cracker squares on a serving dish. Spread 1 heaping tablespoon of cream cheese on each square. Sprinkle each square with ½ teaspoon of sesame seeds and ½ teaspoon of poppy seeds.

3 Place the marshmallows on the prepared baking sheet. Broil them until they're golden brown on top, about 3 minutes. Keep a close eye on them.

4 Place 1 toasted marshmallow on each s'more. Top the s'mores with the remaining graham cracker squares. Serve immediately.

The Infamous S'moresburgers

Once called "totally disgusting in every possible way" on the internet, this meaty s'more is incredibly controversial. Everyone who hasn't eaten one seems to hate the idea with every ounce of their being. I have made s'moresburgers about five different ways in the past five years and, *every time,* I get comments accusing me of stealing the idea from a four-year-old (or a person with a chemically altered brain) to some slightly more aggressive language wishing for my demise via a fiery mallow accident. However, anyone who has ever eaten these burgers loves them. So before you judge, may I just suggest you try these . . . you might be surprised!

This is not a burger you want to serve with a pink center—it's best cooked well done. When you're mixing ground beef with marshmallows and chocolate, even medium-temperature beef is undercooked. **Makes 12 🔥 Takes 30 minutes**

12 ounces ground beef

2 bars (1.55 ounces each) milk chocolate, broken into individual pips

1 tablespoon kosher salt, plus more to taste

Nonstick cooking spray

1 tablespoon extra-virgin olive oil

12 regular marshmallows

12 whole graham crackers, broken in half to form 24 squares

1 Divide the ground beef into 12 equal 1-ounce portions. Place a portion in your palm and flatten it. Place 2 chocolate pips side by side on the flattened patty to form a square in the center of the beef. Wrap the beef around the chocolate and press to seal. Set aside. Repeat with the remaining beef and chocolate.

2 Season the patties aggressively with salt—about ¼ teaspoon per patty, if you want to get technical about it.

3 Place a rack in the upper third of the oven and turn the broiler to its highest setting. Preheat for 5 to 10 minutes. Spray a baking sheet with cooking spray.

4 Meanwhile, heat the olive oil in a medium nonstick skillet over medium-high heat.

5 Add the patties to the skillet (you may need to work in batches). Cook for about 3 minutes. Flip and cook until the patties are brown on both sides and you can see the chocolate just starting to ooze from the center, about 3 minutes more.

6 Place the marshmallows on the prepared baking sheet. Broil them until they're golden brown on top, about 3 minutes. Keep a close eye on them.

7 Place 12 graham cracker squares on a serving dish. Top each square with a cooked patty, 1 toasted marshmallow, and another graham cracker square. Serve immediately.

The Various Personalities of
MARSHMALLOW ROASTERS

5

THE BACK-SEAT ROASTER, much like the fire safety scout, will have lots to say about your marshmallow roasting style. Too close, too far, spin it a little as it cooks, get a longer stick—I think they should worry about their own marshmallow.

Avocado S'mores

I have had a handful of avocado desserts, and what I don't like about most of them is they try to hide the avocado flavor. I put avocado in this s'more because I like the flavor of avocado! Add a pinch of lime and salt and the creamy fruit pairs well with the marshmallow and chocolate. **Makes 12 🔥 Takes 10 minutes**

1 avocado, halved, pitted, peeled, and
  thinly sliced
Pinch of kosher salt
Juice of 1 lime
Nonstick cooking spray

12 whole graham crackers, broken in half
  to form 24 squares
3 bars (1.55 ounces each) milk chocolate,
  broken into individual pips
12 regular marshmallows

1 Place the avocado slices on a plate. Sprinkle with salt and drizzle with the lime juice.

2 Place a rack in the upper third of the oven and turn the broiler to its highest setting. Preheat for 5 to 10 minutes. Spray a baking sheet with cooking spray.

3 Place 12 graham cracker squares on a serving dish. Top each square with 3 chocolate pips. Top the chocolate with 2 or 3 slices of avocado.

4 Place the marshmallows on the prepared baking sheet. Broil them until they're golden brown on top, about 3 minutes. Keep a close eye on them.

5 Place 1 toasted marshmallow on each s'more. Top the s'mores with the remaining graham cracker squares. Serve immediately.

Strawberry Balsamic Mint S'mores

M int is my favorite herb, and it really makes these s'mores. The strawberries soak up the balsamic vinegar and have a nice sweet-sour balance. When you get that hit of fresh mint, though . . . that's where the magic happens.

Makes 12 🔥 **Takes 30 minutes**

12 fresh strawberries, hulled, each cut into 4 to 6 slices

2 tablespoons balsamic vinegar

Pinch of kosher salt

Nonstick cooking spray

12 regular marshmallows

12 whole graham crackers, broken in half to form 24 squares

36 fresh mint leaves

3 bars (1.55 ounces each) milk chocolate, broken into individual pips

1 Gently stir together the strawberries, balsamic vinegar, and salt in a small bowl. Set aside for at least 15 minutes to macerate.

2 Place a rack in the upper third of the oven and turn the broiler to its highest setting. Preheat for 5 to 10 minutes. Spray a baking sheet with cooking spray.

3 Place the marshmallows on the prepared baking sheet. Broil them until they're golden brown on top, about 3 minutes. Keep a close eye on them.

4 Place 12 graham cracker squares on a serving dish. Top each square with 3 mint leaves and 3 chocolate pips.

5 Place 1 toasted marshmallow on each s'more. Spoon 4 to 6 pieces of strawberry over each marshmallow, making sure you get a drizzle of balsamic along with the strawberries. Top the s'mores with the remaining graham cracker squares. Serve immediately.

Prosciutto and Cantaloupe S'mores

Cantaloupe and prosciutto are such a great combo. Two appetizers have inspired this s'more: a melon and prosciutto salad, and breadsticks wrapped in prosciutto. The crunch of the graham cracker, the softness of the melon, and the tear of the prosciutto call to mind both of these dishes as you take a bite. **Makes 12 🔥 Takes 10 minutes**

Nonstick cooking spray

12 regular marshmallows

12 whole graham crackers, broken in half to form 24 squares

3 bars (1.55 ounces each) milk chocolate, broken into individual pips

6 thin prosciutto slices, torn in half

½ cantaloupe, seeded and cut into thin 1½-inch slices

1 Place a rack in the upper third of the oven and turn the broiler to its highest setting. Preheat for 5 to 10 minutes. Spray a baking sheet with cooking spray.

2 Place the marshmallows on the prepared baking sheet. Broil them until they're golden brown on top, about 3 minutes. Keep a close eye on them.

3 Place 12 graham cracker squares on a serving dish. Top each square with 3 chocolate pips, ½ slice of prosciutto, and 2 melon slices.

4 Place 1 toasted marshmallow on each s'more. Top the s'mores with the remaining graham cracker squares. Serve immediately.

Peach, Candied Pecan, and Blue Cheese S'mores

Three s'mores in this book are inspired by salads—of all things—and this is one of them. I wasn't expecting to love this s'more as much as I did, but *wow*. The blue cheese goes so well with the crunchy pecans and the sweet, ripe peaches. The fruit should be so ripe that it melts in your mouth—playing the role that chocolate might play in other s'mores. You can store any leftover candied pecans in an airtight container at room temperature for a month or so. **Makes 12 🔥 Takes 1 hour 30 minutes**

1 large egg white
1 pound (about 4 cups) pecan halves
¾ cup sugar
1 teaspoon kosher salt
½ teaspoon crushed red pepper flakes
Nonstick cooking spray

12 regular marshmallows
12 whole graham crackers, broken in half
      to form 24 squares
2 very ripe peaches, thinly sliced
¾ cup crumbled blue cheese

1 Preheat the oven to 250°F, with a rack in the middle position. Line a baking sheet with a silicone baking mat and set aside.

2 Using a handheld electric mixer, beat the egg white in a medium bowl until frothy, 1 minute. Add the pecan halves to the egg white and stir to combine. Add the sugar, salt, and crushed red pepper flakes. Mix well to coat the pecans. Pour the pecan mixture onto the prepared baking sheet. Bake for 1 hour, stirring every 20 minutes, until the mixture is crunchy. Remove from the oven and set aside.

3 Using oven mitts, place a rack in the upper third of the oven and turn the broiler to its highest setting. Preheat for 5 to 10 minutes. Spray a second baking sheet with cooking spray.

4 Place the marshmallows on the prepared baking sheet. Broil until they're golden brown on top, about 3 minutes. Keep a close eye on them.

5 Place 12 graham cracker squares on a serving dish. If you want crumbles to rival the blue cheese in size, roughly chop the pecans before you add them. Otherwise, top each square with about 5 candied pecans (or the equivalent chopped). Top the pecans with 3 peach slices.

6 Place 1 toasted marshmallow on each s'more, followed by 1 tablespoon of blue cheese. Top the s'mores with the remaining graham cracker squares. Serve immediately.

Plantain Dulce de Leche S'mores

The right plantains are key to these s'mores. They need to be mostly black with a little yellow, otherwise they will taste more like a potato than a sweet, complex banana. The plantains act like nature's crème brûlée—the sugar caramelizes in the pan and the outside gets nice and crispy while the interior remains soft and creamy.

Makes 12 🔥 Takes 20 minutes

2 tablespoons unsalted butter
2 yellow/black plantains, each cut
    on a bias into ½-inch-thick slices,
    12 slices total
Nonstick cooking spray

12 whole graham crackers, broken in half
    to form 24 squares
1 cup dulce de leche
12 regular marshmallows

1   Melt the butter in a skillet over medium heat. Add the plantain slices. Cook, flipping once halfway through the cooking time, to brown both sides, about 8 minutes total. Remove from the heat and set aside.

2   Place a rack in the upper third of the oven and turn the broiler to its highest setting. Preheat for 5 to 10 minutes. Spray a baking sheet with cooking spray.

3   Place 12 graham cracker squares on the prepared baking sheet. Top each square with 1 heaping tablespoon of dulce de leche and 1 plantain slice. Squish each marshmallow a bit with your hands and place 1 marshmallow on each plantain slice. Broil until the marshmallows are golden brown on top, about 3 minutes. Keep a close eye on them.

4   Transfer the s'mores to a serving dish and top with the remaining graham cracker squares. Serve immediately.

Fig and Brie S'mores

I first tried putting these fig and Brie s'mores on a more savory cracker, but I soon discovered that having the actual graham cracker made them feel more like s'mores, and, not only that, the sweetness of the fig jam really pairs well with the graham. These are best served as part of a charcuterie board or an antipasti platter. **Makes 12 🔥 Takes 15 minutes**

Nonstick cooking spray
2 wedges (6 ounces each) Brie,
    rind left on, each cut into 6 cubes
    (12 total)

12 whole graham crackers, broken in half
      to form 24 squares
¾ cup fig jam

1 Place a rack in the upper third of the oven and turn the broiler to its highest setting. Preheat for 5 to 10 minutes. Spray a baking sheet with cooking spray.

2 Arrange the Brie cubes on the prepared baking sheet. Broil the cheese until browned, about 5 minutes. Flip and broil until the cheese is browned on both sides, about 5 minutes more. Keep a close eye on the cheese.

3 Place 12 graham cracker squares on a serving dish. Top each square with 1 tablespoon of fig jam, 1 toasted Brie cube, and another graham cracker square. Press down lightly to secure. Serve immediately.

Antipasto
S'mores

When you serve these little antipasto sandwiches and call them s'mores, no one will question you. They look so much like s'mores! The goat cheese "marshmallow" is just so perfect with the flavorful olive salad and the salty, crispy salami. **Makes 12 🔥 Takes 20 minutes**

Nonstick cooking spray

¾ cup minced green olives

1 tablespoon chopped fresh parsley

½ garlic clove, grated

Juice of 1 lemon

24 salami slices

1 log (8 ounces) goat cheese, cut into
    12 rounds

. . . .

1   Preheat the oven to 350°F, with a rack in the middle position. Spray a baking sheet with cooking spray and set aside.

2   Mix the olives, parsley, garlic, and lemon juice in a small bowl. Gently stir to combine and set aside.

3   Place the salami on the prepared baking sheet. Bake the salami until crispy, about 12 minutes.

4   Transfer 12 pieces of salami to a serving dish. Top each salami with 1 goat cheese round, 1 tablespoon of the olive mixture, and another piece of salami. Serve immediately.

SMORS D'OEUVRES

You may have noticed that things have taken a turn here, right as we are about to end this book. Lest the delicious Antipasto S'more on the left take you by surprise, may I suggest referring back to The Rules of S'more (page iii), number four: "No matter how far away you get from the traditional s'more . . . it must visually look like a s'more." So now that you've known almost fifty other ways to s'more, it's time to let your imagination run wild. The white foods below are suggestions for ingredients that look like (or can be made to resemble) marshmallows. Take your melon baller to the veggies, if necessary. For a bit of s'mores whimsy, make sure to have a friendly polar bear on hand to serve and a decorative jar of cotton balls.

Pair these with the cracker and sauce, pesto, dip, or spread of your choice:

- Any small ball of cheese
- White mushroom caps stuffed with breadcrumbs or sausage
- Roasted cauliflower core
- Grilled tofu
- Glazed or roasted turnips
- Mascarpone
- Dollop of sour cream

Caprese S'mores

Caprese salad is such a ubiquitous and popular appetizer, and, because mozzarella looks so much like a marshmallow, it took me about 3 seconds to realize this would be a great twist on a s'more. Like any s'more, though, give the cheese a nice char before placing it on the cracker! **Makes 12 Takes 15 minutes**

Nonstick cooking spray

¼ cup chopped fresh basil

¼ cup olive oil

12 pearl-size fresh mozzarella balls, or
    3 larger balls cut into 1-inch cubes

24 focaccia-style crackers

5 to 10 grape tomatoes, thinly sliced

1   Place a rack in the upper third of the oven and turn the broiler to its highest setting. Preheat for 5 to 10 minutes. Spray a baking sheet with cooking spray.

2   Mix the basil with the olive oil in a small bowl and let it infuse for 10 minutes.

3   Place the mozzarella balls on the prepared baking sheet. Broil the mozzarella until brown and splotchy, about 7 minutes.

4   Place 12 crackers on a serving dish. Top each cracker with at least 1 slice of tomato and 1 toasted mozzarella ball. Drizzle about 2 teaspoons of the basil oil over each s'more. Top the s'mores with the remaining crackers. Serve immediately.

Scallop, Zucchini, and Pesto S'mores

Seven years ago, I saw a scallop on a skewer while I was in my parents' backyard. I was about to roast some marshmallows with my friends when I looked over and saw my mom lining up a few white, fluffy morsels on a skewer. At first, I thought, *well, that's a clever way to roast several marshmallows at once.* When I realized the grilled scallops had fooled me, I became obsessed with coming up with ideas for foods that looked like s'mores but were made with completely different ingredients. Little did I know it would be the first step down a long road that would eventually lead to a whole book of insane s'mores twists. **Makes 12 🔥 Takes 30 minutes**

12 fresh sea scallops
Kosher salt
Freshly ground black pepper
Olive oil, for drizzling

1 small zucchini, sliced into 12 thin rounds
4 naan rounds, about the size of a tortilla
¾ cup prepared pesto

1 Soak two long wooden skewers in warm water for 30 minutes. Thread 6 scallops on each of the skewers. Season with salt and pepper and drizzle with olive oil.

2 Drizzle the zucchini rounds with olive oil and season with salt and pepper.

3 Heat a grill to high or heat a grill pan over high heat.

4 Place the skewered scallops, zucchini rounds, and naan rounds on the grill. Grill the zucchini until it is softened and charred slightly, 1 minute per side. Grill the naan on both sides to blacken and crisp up slightly, about 2 minutes per side. Grill the scallops until they are brown on both sides, about 3 minutes per side. As they are done, transfer the grilled items to a wire rack or cutting board to cool.

5 Cut each naan into 6 square or round crackers, 24 pieces total, and place them on a serving plate.

6 Place 1 zucchini round on 12 of the naan crackers. Top each zucchini round with 1 scallop, followed by 1 tablespoon of the pesto. Top the s'mores with the remaining naan crackers. Serve immediately.

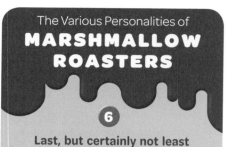

The Various Personalities of

MARSHMALLOW ROASTERS

6

Last, but certainly not least in our Roasters Roundup, is **THE GORDMALLOW RAMSAY.** This meticulous roaster will pull out all the techniques to get their marshmallow the perfect shade of golden brown on all edges and soft and creamy in the center—closer to the fire, farther from the fire, with a gentle breath of air to cool things down when they get too hot. And they will always stake out the optimal location to roast, with good convection coming from all directions.

Index

Note: Page references in italics indicate photographs.